SAINTS FOR OUR TIMES

Jerome K. Williams

Augustine Institute

Greenwood Village, CO

Augustine Institute
6160 S. Syracuse Way, Suite 310
Greenwood Village, CO 80111
Tel: (866) 767-3155
www.augustineinstitute.org

Cover Design: Devin Schadt
Cover Image: © Restored Traditions. Used by Permission.

Excerpted from *True Reformers: Saints of the Catholic Reformation*
© 2017 Augustine Institute, Greenwood Village, CO
ISBN-978-0-9982041-8-5
All rights reserved.
Printed in the United States of America

Contents

Foreword

There are no cookie-cutter saints. The saint is living proof that God has made each of us in his own image and completely unique. One can lose this sense of distinctiveness when reading about the saints. They all begin to look the same—in prayer and penance, in miracles, and in pious phrases and/or summaries of their teaching that border on truisms.

Not so with the *Saints for Our Times*.

In the pages that follow are depictions of four saints who were all completely committed to Christ and his Church and yet were completely different. These are testimonies to the uniqueness of every human being, a uniqueness that only becomes clearer as the saint is conformed to Christ.

Here there are no clichéd phrases that could be applied to every holy person who ever lived. Each of the depictions of the saints comes alive as the story of an individual. In a few pages, one understands what it means for Francis Xavier to travel the world with a missionary spirit. We learn to understand Ignatius of Loyola's conversion from soldier to pilgrim. We catch a glimpse of the mystical soul of St. Teresa and incredible resilience of St. John of the Cross. To read these accounts is a kind of retreat. It provides an opportunity to reflect on *our* love of God, *our* prayer life, and the mission God has given each of us in light of our spiritual teachers.

In *Saints for Our Times*, we see the missions of these saints in relation to the needs of the Church and the world.

In fact, the diagnoses of the times teach something profound about the Church and the world and allow us to see how the spirit of the saint meets the distinctive needs of the day. In this there is contemporary application for the reader. It has one asking: Where are the saints that God is raising up today that I may follow them?

Although each of these saints is remarkable for their uniqueness, I was struck by a constant refrain in all of them. Each was deeply committed to the humble and difficult task of serving Christ in the poor and needy. They all served in hospitals—a very different kind of institution then than now—or during plagues. And, they gave generously of their things and time to the poor, not occasionally as a kind of spiritual recreation or as an obligation of office, but as an expression of love that burst forth from their life of discipleship. It offers a challenge to each of us who are finding our way along the road to holiness—do we love Christ in the poor? Does it cost us?

These saints were not perfect people. Many of their plans did not come off, certain decisions they took certainly look as though they could have been taken differently to better effect. They were real men and women, not idealizations. They remain windows to God, and their transcendent love comes through, but not in a way that makes them strange. Rather they are like us. And as such they inspire us because, we may dare to believe, that if they are like us, then we can be like them.

Jonathan J. Reyes
Executive Director USCCB Department of Justice,
Peace, and Human Development

Introduction

"Humans must be changed by religion,
not religion by humans."
—Giles of Viterbo, Fifth Lateran Council, 1512

The saints are the glory of the Church. They are the clearest expression of the Church's divine mission and life-transforming power, and the surest sign of hope for those who are walking the homeward road in their company.

A question often asked is whether or not Christianity "works." Can its claims be believed? Has it made good on its promises? Does it represent a successful attempt at ordering human affairs? Often these days the sharply returned answer is "no!" Our age is keenly aware and highly critical of the sins and faults of former times, occasionally even with accuracy. There are many who take issue with the Church, claiming that Christianity has been a failure. Their case is well prepared. For starters, look at the periods of so-called Christian society: one need not go through the litany of alleged faults, from the Crusades to the Inquisition to Galileo; they are repeated so often as to have become catchphrases. Then further, look at the history of the institutional Church itself. Often among the leaders of the Church—bishops and priests and monks and nuns—examples of greed, sensuality, and desire for power are not hard to find. Even where more blatant sins are not in evidence, there often lurks a spirit of small-mindedness, of pettiness and selfishness, rather than the large-hearted, noble, and generous spirit promised by the Gospel. What happened to the high Christian ideal of restoring all things, of forming a new kind of human being, of participating in divine power, of loving one another with supernatural help? Then the gaze shifts to the present. It is easy to find examples of bad behavior among Catholics, from the scandalous activity of misbehaving priests to the less sensational but more common experience of lukewarmness and hypocrisy among the laity. Doesn't all of this point to a failed idea? However much we may admire the personality of Jesus, and whatever positive qualities the theoretical vision of Christianity may possess, has not the Church shown itself incapable of making real what it so eloquently professes?

An essential aspect of the Church as founded by Christ is that it is both a divine and a human institution. This combination of humanity and divinity, a mixture that has often been found offensive to spiritually sensitive people, is God's preferred mode of artistry. He takes up the theme in whatever he does, weaving together in indescribable ways matter and spirit, the mortal and the immortal, the Creator and the creature, in all his great works. The mixture can be seen in his conception of the human, this odd being composed of both body and spirit, bound by time and space but with a capacity and a corresponding longing for a divine destiny. The theme shows up in the way God brought forth his written word, the Sacred Scriptures, writings of varied forms and languages generated over more than a thousand years, penned by many different hands and minds—all very human processes—yet nonetheless authored by the Holy Spirit and possessing a divine quality and an authority unlike any other book. The theme is expressed most forcibly, even shockingly, in the union of the divine Son of God, the Eternal Logos, with a specific human being at a particular time and place, Creator and creature locked in a mysterious unity. And the theme takes form in the Church, a visible institution with every possible kind of human aspect—governmental, relational, cultural, economic, organizational—made up of and run by flawed men and women, yet mysteriously the very Body of Christ present in the world.

The saints are given to us in order to perceive this mystery at work. It is in their shining example that the promises of God to renew the human race are made most visible.

This understanding of the true state of humanity can help in assessing one popular current of thought that calls Christianity a failure. Much of the intensity of this sentiment comes from the essentially utopian attitude of most of our contemporaries. Having denied Original Sin, our society is left thinking that we really can fundamentally fix the world. So we set out to eradicate injustice, greed, lust for power, trafficking in humans, even sadness and loneliness, and we put forward our plans to fashion a world of peace, happiness, and justice. Seen through this lens, Christianity is thought to be one among a number of programs designed to accomplish these utopian goals; and from this point of view, the results of two thousand years of Christianity are far from overwhelming. The influence of the Church on whole cultures and civilizations can hardly be denied, yet we seem no closer to our envisaged paradise than we were before Christ arrived. Christianity is thus judged to have been a failure, because it has not decisively eradicated the evils that have beset us.

But this is a profound misunderstanding of what Christianity has claimed to do and to be. Christ did not come to turn the earth into a paradise—not yet. Christians have never believed that all evil, or even most of it, could be overcome in the current age of the world. Christ came "to bear witness to the truth" (Jn 18:37), and from the beginning of salvation history the evidence is not great that humans on the whole have desired truth. At his birth, Jesus was spoken of by Simeon as "the fall and rising of many" and a sign of contradiction (Lk 2:34). The Church is accomplishing her mission when she is true to her Founder, when she bears witness to the truth of Christ, and when she helps those who desire Christ along a path of healing and of hope in a coming Kingdom. Jesus himself was not universally hailed and honored; quite the opposite.

How then is the success or failure of the Church to be assessed most clearly? The measure of her success will be found in the personalities of the saints, her truest and most representative members. The saints are those who rise with Christ; they are examples of the kind of transformation possible for those who are willing to take the Divine Doctor at his word, and who are ready to follow his prescriptions. They are a sure sign of the continuing presence of Christ in the world.

In matters of reform, the saints are once again decisive. True reform is a matter of regaining and maintaining the true image of Christ, and the true reformer is the one who most fully expresses the image of Christ in all facets of life. It has been said that the Church is not a democracy; it has often come almost as an accusation that the Church does not settle matters of truth, justice, or goodness by majority vote. But if the Church is not a democracy, she is not a monarchy either, not in the usual sense of that word. True,

Christ is the King, the Head of his Body, and in that sense the Church is gloriously monarchical. But in putting Christ's kingship into action through the ministries of his servants, in matters of polity, in making her way through the world, in sorting out the many issues and challenges she faces in a constantly changing human environment, the Church operates neither as a monarchy nor as a democracy. She moves forward mysteriously as a kind of oligarchy of the influence of the saints. When all is said and done, when the dust of the frenzied moment settles, when the broad lines of the Church's life can be traced through time, an astonishing truth emerges. The Church has not simply gone the way of her popes, or her bishops, or her theologians, or her councils, or the majority of her believing members. Instead, the Church has followed her saints; and when she has followed popes or bishops or theologians, she has done so especially when they were saints, or because they were following the tracks marked out by saints. The Church will be found to have kept careful tabs, by an ineffable spiritual sense, on those remarkable responders to the grace of God. "Be imitators of me, as I am of Christ," said St. Paul to the Corinthians (1 Cor 11:1). So the Corinthians did; and so the Church has done down through the centuries, imitating those imitators of Christ, the saints.

This means that if we want to comprehend the essence of the Church, we need to become acquainted with her most characteristic members, the saints. If we want evidence of the transformative power of the Gospel, we should seek it in the lives of those who took the Gospel most seriously: the saints. If we want to understand the nature of true reform, we will find its pattern in the lives and in the teaching of the true reformers of the Church: the saints.

The sixteenth century, the time during which the reforming saints chronicled in this book lived, was for Europe an age of profound change. The medieval system that had pertained for many centuries was breaking down. European society was being altered in significant ways—demographically, economically, politically, and geographically—in a process that was putting a great strain on existing institutions. Populations were rapidly growing and a new educated and literate middle class was emerging. New centers of cultural and political power were gathering at the courts of European monarchies. The invention of the printing press made the Scriptures and other spiritual writings easily accessible and whetted the appetite of the age for greater theological clarity and consistency. A renewed and deepened encounter with classical civilization through the recovery of many ancient texts was creating a ferment in the mind of the age. A higher standard was being demanded in many areas of life, not least in that most important area of all: religion. At the same time, Christendom was hard-pressed to protect itself from an increasingly potent Ottoman empire and was both challenged and intoxicated as the worlds of Asia and the Americas came into its vision. In the midst of this seething change, the key institution of society, the Church, was in dire need of reform. Old patterns were no longer working; old arrangements that had once served their turn were proving ineffective or corrupting. For a number of generations, the call had been voiced by all serious believers: "Reform in head and members!"

Historians have observed that revolutions most often occur, not when things are at their dismal worst, but rather during times of rising expectations. In such times, what had been previously at least an adequate state of affairs no longer satisfies the higher standards of a new age. The sixteenth century was just such a time of rising expectations in religious matters, and of a loss of patience with problems in the path of reform. It was an age of deep religious faith and great religious ferment, of strong and colorful personalities who responded to God amid the circumstances of their time in ways that continue to influence the Church and the world to this day.

Among the most remarkable of those personalities were the four saints in this volume, whose lives exemplify the way Church reform was furthered by lay men and women, priests, contemplatives, bishops, and popes. Seeing how they responded to the challenges of their age will help us to understand the times in which they lived—and more than that, hopefully it will be an inspiration and a source of wisdom for meeting the demands of our own rapidly changing and highly challenging age.

Chapter One

St. Ignatius Loyola

"Go and set the world on fire!"

The year 1492 is famous to Americans as the year Columbus discovered the New World, sailing under the patronage of the Spanish crown. It has yet another significance in Spanish history. It was the year of the final expulsion of the Moors from the Iberian Peninsula, the last act in a drama that had been unfolding for centuries, and it marked the beginning of what has been called *El Siglo de Oro,* Spain's Golden Age. First under the joint rule of Ferdinand and Isabella, and then during the reign of Charles V, Spain emerged as Europe's strongest kingdom and the world's first global power. The Spaniards developed a vast empire, controlling large portions of Europe and ruling lands from Latin America and Africa to the Philippines in East Asia. The Spanish army during those years was well-nigh invincible. Yet not only in political life, but in all areas of cultural activity, sixteenth-century Spain saw a remarkable efflorescence. This was the age of El Greco and Velazquez in painting, of Cervantes and Lope de Vega in literature, of Tomas de Victoria in music. It was a time of the growth of universities and of rich developments in many branches of learning. The Spanish were a proud people: proud of their military talent, of their chivalric customs, of their cultural achievements, and of their allegiance to the Catholic

Faith. Having been forged in a centuries-long fight for their national and religious identity, they characteristically pursued their aims with great energy, courage, and determination. A national character of this type could be a double-edged sword. It might, if unredeemed, produce the vainglorious conquistador or the haughty courtier. But when transformed by the love of God, it could also prove fertile soil for a very high type of sanctity.

It is a truth about saints that they transcend the age in which they live. Each generation discovers them anew and finds fresh inspiration in their lives and their example. But it is also true that saints are human characters embedded in the possibilities and limitations of their times. They are not strange prodigies alien to the spirit of their age, but men and women who, by their cooperation with God's initiative, have allowed the whole of their personalities and all the elements of their inherited culture to be touched by grace and thus lifted and purified. In the lives of the saints, as in everything else, grace builds on nature.[1] This truth is clearly at work in the figure of Ignatius Loyola. He was a Spanish hidalgo of Basque descent, and in many respects his approach to God and to the spiritual life reflected his background. At the same time, under the transforming hand of God, the qualities typical of his country and class gained in Ignatius a universal meaning.

Iñigo was born in 1491, the youngest of thirteen children, in the ancestral castle of the Loyolas, a Basque family of minor nobility. (He would take the name Ignatius later in life, perhaps in imitation of the martyr Ignatius of Antioch.) Of his early life we have little detail beyond a few reminiscences taken down many years later. At around

---

[1] Cf. Thomas Aquinas, *Summa Theologica*, Part 1, 1:8: "Grace does not destroy nature but perfects it."

age fifteen, he took service as a page in the household of a relative who had a significant post in the kingdom of Castile. In his mid-twenties he entered military service under the Viceroy of Navarre. The military vocation came naturally to Ignatius; he came from a family of soldiers. One of his brothers died fighting in Mexico City, a second in Naples, and a third against the Turks in Hungary. Ignatius imbibed deeply of the spirit of his time and place, and set before his eyes the ideal of the accomplished man of the world: vain and dashing, concerned with military glory and the attentions of fashionable ladies. His brief comment in his *Autobiography* (in which he speaks of himself in the third person) notes simply that "he was a man given over to vanities of the world with a great and vain desire to win fame."[2] In his military capacity under the Viceroy, in the year 1521, he had the task of leading the defense of the fortress of Pamplona against a French attack. It was characteristic of the man to insist on defending the fort even when his comrades-in-arms thought it indefensible. In the midst of battle, he was hit by a cannonball that badly broke one of his legs and wounded the other. With their valiant captain down, the defense of the fort collapsed, and Ignatius was sent by his courteous French captors to convalesce at the home of his father. His insistence that his leg be healed such as not to mar his appearance led to a number of painful operations, and at times he was close to death. He was thirty years old, and his life was about to take a radical new direction.

To pass the time while convalescing, Ignatius asked to be given books of chivalrous romances. There were none of the kind he wanted to be found in the castle, so instead he took to

---

[2] St. Ignatius of Loyola, *The Autobiography of St. Ignatius of Loyola*, trans. Joseph O'Callaghan, ed. John C. Olin (New York: Fordham University Press, 1992), 21.

reading two religious books: *The Life of Christ* by the German monk Ludolph of Saxony, and *The Golden Legend*, a collection of the lives of the saints. Confronted by the personality of Christ and the great deeds of the saints, Ignatius was deeply moved. All the Spanish chivalric instinct and desire for glory that ran so strongly in him were caught up and inflamed; his earlier desire for worldly fame was transposed into a determination to do great things for his true King and so to win honor in Heaven. "While reading the life of Our Lord and of the saints," Ignatius remembered later, "he stopped to think, reasoning within himself, 'What if I should do what St. Francis did, what St. Dominic did?'"[3] He was filled with loathing for his past life, and he determined to do penance by taking to the road as a pilgrim. It was the beginning of a long journey that would ultimately have a great effect on both the Church and the world.

The year 1521 was notable for more than Ignatius's conversion. It was the year that Hernán Cortés, a man of roughly the same age and social background as Ignatius, completed the conquest of Tenochtitlán and the Aztec Empire, opening a new chapter in Spanish and European history. It was also the year in which Martin Luther, having written three widely-read tracts against the Catholic Church, refused to retract his positions before the imperial general assembly, or Diet, at Worms, thereby effectively initiating the Protestant Reformation. These momentous events did much to shape the world into which Ignatius would throw his considerable energies as a missionary and reformer of the Church. He later said, "I do not consider myself as having retired from military service, but only as having come under the orders of God."

[3] *Ibid*, 23.

Ignatius's life after his conversion can conveniently be divided into three parts or phases, each of which has its special significance. The first phase, which began as soon as his conversion had commenced, lasted some three years. It included the time of his convalescence, his yearlong stay in Manresa, and his pilgrimage to the Holy Land. This was a period of intense interior life: long hours of prayer, rigorous works of penance and purification, and remarkable mystical experiences. The second phase, lasting some fourteen years, was an extended time of study and apostolic activity during which Ignatius gathered groups of men around him, first in Barcelona, then at the universities of Alcalá, Salamanca, and Paris, and then for a short time in Venice. It was a period of honing his method of evangelization and of significant opposition to his apostolate. The final phase began with his return to Rome in 1538 and involved the founding of the Society of Jesus two years later and his wide-ranging duties as general of the order, a task that ended only with his death in 1556.

The First Phase: Ignatius Is Taught by God

A time-honored practical rule of the spiritual life says that one needs to be careful when imitating the saints. Their faith, their virtues, and their abandonment to the Divine Will are examples for all believers. But the particular patterns of their lives and the specific ways they are called to respond to providential initiative are often exceptional and idiosyncratic. What is excellent in the life of a saint may not be prudent or praiseworthy in every believer. This rule should be remembered when we examine the life of St. Ignatius.

From the time of his initial conversion, Ignatius was dealt with by God in a unique way. The uniqueness was not so much

in the conversion itself. It was certainly a dramatic event to
go from soldier to pilgrim as Ignatius did, leaving behind
family, worldly ambitions, social status, and possessions in
order to follow Christ. But many others caught by the beauty
and love of God have altered their lives in equally drastic
ways. When Peter and John left their nets and their fishing
business to follow Jesus, they modeled the inner pattern of
every true conversion. What made the early years of Ignatius's
conversion so distinctive was the degree to which God took
him in hand and taught him profound spiritual and pastoral
truths, including the whole cycle of Catholic doctrine, in a
way almost entirely unmediated by the help of others. Ignatius
himself came to realize this. He later said of those first years:
"God treated him at this time just as a schoolmaster treats
a child whom he is teaching…he clearly believed and has
always believed that God treated him in this way."[4]

There was a clear providential purpose in the conversion
of Ignatius. Like St. Paul, Ignatius was a chosen instrument
to be used by Christ for the sake of a great apostolic mission.
Like Paul, he had a strong personality and an iron will,
but these traits were being exercised in a wrong direction.
Like Paul, he was taught the Gospel by the Holy Spirit as a
preparation for that mission. Paul once wrote of his own
reception of the Faith: "Brethren, I would have you know that
the gospel which was preached by me is not man's gospel.
For I did not receive it from man, nor was I taught it, but
it came through a revelation of Jesus Christ" (Gal 1:11–12).
Though never claiming any special prophetic or apostolic
authority, Ignatius spoke similarly about his own manner of
receiving the Gospel. He later recounted an experience of this

---

[4] *Autobiography*, 37.

kind from his time at Manresa: "While he was seated there, the eyes of his understanding began to be opened; though he did not see any vision, he understood and knew many things, both spiritual things and matters of faith and of learning." Along with this experience of infused understanding, Ignatius received visions of Christ, Our Lady, and the Trinity that so deeply impressed the truths of the faith upon him that, as he later said, "if there were no Scriptures to teach us these matters of the faith, he would be resolved to die for them, only because of what he had seen."[5]

The effect of these divine visions and graces was evident in the way Ignatius began, soon after his conversion, not only to talk about his newfound life, which would have been natural enough, but to lead others confidently as a teacher of the Faith and a director of souls. From a distance of time and a knowledge of his future course, it seems obvious that Ignatius would quickly have become a spiritual guide. But if we see him as he would have been viewed by his contemporaries, the strangeness of his behavior is more arresting. Here was a man who had spent the whole of his thirty years pursuing nothing but worldly interests. He had thrown all his energy into the acquisition of fame and a prestigious career, and his tastes and affections had been molded on that pattern. He was no doubt a Catholic, but of that common hereditary type who was familiar with the cultural practices of the Church but viewed them as mere social conventions. Well-trained in military arts and in the demands of polite society, he was otherwise poorly educated. He knew next to nothing of theology. This same man then has a dramatic encounter with Christ and determines to change the course of his life. He has

[5] *Ibid*, 39.

a necessarily arduous business before him, the task of every convert who has been busily shaping his character apart from the will of God. He will need to unlearn the ingrained habits of many years. He will need to develop a new set of spiritual senses to come alive to invisible realities. He will need to learn something of the rich body of doctrine and practice that every serious Catholic embraces. He can expect, even as he counts on God's help, that this will require time and hard work, and he will need good teachers and mentors to help him along the way.

But under the impulse of grace, Ignatius takes an entirely different path. Though he seeks spiritual mentors, he can find no one who suits his need. Instead, he is drawn into an intense solitary experience of being trained directly by the hand of God, schooled in the truths of the Faith and in principles of prayer and rules of discernment. He then confidently takes others under his wing as a spiritual master and teaches them what he has learned, though he is only the merest beginner in the spiritual life. This sort of behavior would typically characterize an overzealous neophyte with more enthusiasm than knowledge. But such was not the case with Ignatius. Though an untrained layman, he displayed a sure grasp of the doctrinal and moral truths of the Faith. The novel method of conversion and discipleship that he developed during these solitary years, the so-called Spiritual Exercises, quickly came to be recognized as a marvel of Catholic spirituality and have been counted among the most effective means of spiritual transformation that the Church has known. All this from a man who had never studied theology, had never been guided by a spiritual director, and until the day before yesterday had been leading the life of a vain worldling. Those who witnessed the spectacle might well have asked themselves the same question posed by the astonished townspeople of Nazareth as they listened to the teaching of Jesus: "Where then did this man get all this?" (Mt 13:56).

The Pauline-like conversion and early experience of Ignatius underlines a key principle of Church reform: namely, that Christ is Lord of the Church, and it is he who takes the initiative in imparting and protecting the divine life of his Body. The sixteenth-century Church was in dire need of reform, and serious Christians were rightly concerned about what they might do to rectify matters. But the fortunes of the Church depend ultimately not on human activity—however important that may be—but on the faithfulness of God. If the instruments that are meant to care for Christ's Church and his mission prove faulty, he will find others suited to his purposes, even if it means catching hold of a wounded middle-aged Basque soldier.

The Second Phase: Apostolic Success and Opposition

From first to last, Ignatius was a man of deeds. He put a high value on prayer, and his own spiritual life puts him in the company of the Church's great mystics; but like an arrow on a string, he was always poised and ready to fly into action. The question he posed to himself and to his spiritual disciples was always: What will we do for Christ and his greater glory? Ignatius's first thought upon his conversion was that he would go on pilgrimage to the Holy Land. There had been a long tradition of pilgrimage as a penitential exercise, and to this purpose Ignatius added a deeper motive. Knowing that his life was now taking a different course as a disciple of Christ, he hoped to remain in the Holy Land and to serve other pilgrims at the holy sites and, if possible, to preach the Gospel among the Turks. After his stay at Manresa, he set off for the Near East, and through many adventures and difficulties he arrived in Jerusalem. But it soon became clear that the Franciscan keepers of the holy sites would not give him permission to remain. After less than a month in the Holy City, he was obliged to take ship again for home. He later recounted, "After the pilgrim realized that it was not God's will that he remain in Jerusalem, he continually pondered within himself what he ought to do. At last he inclined more to study for some time so he would be able to help souls."[6]

During this new phase of his life, Ignatius pursued his studies, but by his own account his education was not the main thing occupying his mind and his energies. The universities he attended were among the most prominent of his time—the University of Alcalá, recently founded by the great humanist scholar and Church reformer Cardinal Ximenes, where he spent a year and a half; the University of Salamanca, Spain's most famous university, where he stayed for six months; and finally the University of Paris, the premier theological school of Christendom, where he studied for seven years and eventually became a master of theology. But though his education was necessary to him as a tool for his mission, it was not an important chapter in the formation of his understanding or his spiritual life. He had already imbibed the truths of the Faith in a profound way by supernatural means. He later commented that what he had learned directly from God at Manresa, before he had begun his formal education, was of such richness and depth that "in

[6] *Ibid*, 54.

the whole course of his life, through sixty-two years, even if he gathered up all the many helps he had had from God and all the many things he knew and added them together, he does not think they would amount to as much as he had received at that one time."[7]

What did occupy Ignatius's mind and energy during these years, apart from the time-consuming task of begging for his livelihood, was his apostolic outreach. Here again one sees a likeness to the Apostle Paul. Like Paul, Ignatius had a burning desire to preach the Gospel, what he described as being "of use to souls." Like Paul, Ignatius was warm-hearted and passionate, making a deep impression on all those he met. Like Paul, he was not a skilled speaker: he never really mastered any language beyond his own native Basque, and his preaching and conversation in Castilian, French, or Italian were often peppered with grammatical errors and a mixture of words from different tongues. Like Paul, wherever he went he brought about rapid conversions and raised a storm of turbulence. A regular pattern began to occur: first, there would be public notice of him; then a number of conversions to the Faith; and then growing resistance to his apostolate.

It is not surprising that Ignatius would make a splash wherever he went. A man of the noble class, already in his mid-thirties, he arrived at the university to study with men half his age. Though a layman, he wore a hermit's garb of rough fabric, went barefoot, and begged alms to meet his daily necessities. He spent much of his time praying and was regular and devout in his reception of the sacraments. He took whatever opportunity he could to speak about the

---

[7] *Ibid*, 39–40.

service of God, and, by all accounts, despite his unusual way of living—perhaps because of it—he was highly effective. He invited those who responded favorably to his message to take the Spiritual Exercises, and the results were often dramatic. Many, some among them of high station, would take a renewed interest in serving God and seriously alter their lives, and there was always a handful of young men who would join him, throwing over their secular ambitions and imitating his life and his apostolic work. At a certain point, all this ferment would spark a reaction. Whether from a genuine concern for the good of the Church, or from jealousy of his influence, or from worldly motives among relatives of his converts who were worried at the readiness of his disciples to abandon wealth and position, his apostolic activity would be attacked. By some, he was called a seducer of students; others questioned his orthodoxy; others spread false rumors about his morals and called his companions "sack-wearers" and "illuminati." On more than one occasion, he was imprisoned. Five times he came before the Inquisition, and five times it was found that there was no error either in his doctrine or in his way of life. He carried himself through all these ordeals with calm fervor. "Does imprisonment seem such a great evil to you?" he said to a woman who expressed concern once at finding him in jail. "I will tell you that there are not so many grills and chains in Salamanca that I would not wish for more for the love of God."[8]

The great instrument of Ignatius's apostolic work was the Spiritual Exercises that he first developed at Manresa and continued to hone as the years went by. Much has been written about the Exercises, which comprise not so much a book of

[8] *Ibid*, 70.

devotion as a manual for making a thirty-day retreat. The point of the Exercises was to take the retreatant out of the normal stream of life and during a prolonged and intensive period set before him the great truths of the Faith, using for the purpose many different means: meditation on the Scripture, strong appeals to the imagination, familiar prayer, external austerities and supports, regular examination of conscience, the pursuit of particular virtues, and frequent reception of the sacraments. The Exercises were intended to result not only in conversion but also in a determination to pattern the whole of life for the glory of God and the good of others. Ignatius had great confidence in the power of the Exercises to effect serious change and would use whatever means he could to bring his friends and disciples to them. Once he made a wager with a friend who was vacillating about taking the month-long plunge. He suggested they play a game of billiards; the loser would do whatever the winner wanted for thirty days. They played, and Ignatius won. The man went through the Exercises and had a complete change of life.

The Exercises provided the age with something many were seeking: a way of approaching the spiritual life that was at the same time explosively potent and eminently practical. Their manner of promoting an intimate personal connection with Christ appealed to a time that was putting more emphasis on individual experience. The Exercises left an indelible imprint on the sixteenth-century reform of the Church. Ignatius wrote of them many years later: "The Spiritual Exercises are the best that I have been able to think out, experience, and understand in this life, both for helping somebody to make the most of themselves, as also for being able to bring advantage, help, and profit to many others."[9]

[9] Ignatius to Fr. Miona, 16 November 1536, in *St. Ignatius of Loyola: Personal Writings*, trans. Joseph A. Munitiz and Philip Endean, (New York: Penguin, 1996), 139.

Two aspects of the Exercises can be underlined as giving a sense of the whole. One was what Ignatius called the "Principle and Foundation." Ignatius focused the mind with a laser-like intensity on the purpose of human life and insisted that everything be seen and judged in the light of that purpose. "Man is created to praise, reverence, and serve God our Lord, and by this means to save his soul. All other things on the face of the earth are created for man to help him fulfill the end for which he is created." This being the case, one should use the things of the world insofar as they helped to attain that end, and rid oneself of all that might get in the way. All desire and all choice should be directed to "attaining the end for which we are created."[10]

A second key aspect of the Exercises was a way of imaginatively viewing life best expressed in the meditation on "The Two Standards." Ignatius had the disciple imagine, by a careful construction of an interior picture, two armies arrayed for battle: one led by Lucifer, the other led by Christ. Lucifer was pictured as "seated on a great throne of fire and smoke, in the center of the vast plain of Babylon," surrounded by countless demons whom he scattered across the world "to ensnare men and to bind them in chains." It was "a horrible and terrible sight to behold." By contrast, Christ was standing in a lowly place around Jerusalem, "beautiful and gracious." Christ was choosing disciples, and he sent them "throughout the whole world to spread his sacred doctrine among men of every state and condition."[11] Both Lucifer and Christ wanted all men under their standard; each called them to follow him; a great battle was waging between them. The momentous question posed by the Exercises was: Whose standard will you take

[10] *Ibid.*, 289.
[11] *Ibid*, 310–11.

up? Under which banner will you fight? There was no middle ground; one had to choose one side or the other.

The image of the disciple as a valiant soldier fighting under a glorious captain may have had a special appeal to the former soldier in Ignatius, but it was not his own invention. It was an image rooted in the Scripture and with a long tradition in Christian spirituality. But under the hand of Ignatius that image gained a vivid and motivating clarity. Ignatius would later write to young aspirants of the Society:

> Place before your eyes as models for your imitation, not the cowardly and the weak, but the brave and the fervent. Blush to be surpassed by the children of the world, who are more solicitous to acquire the goods of time than you are to gain the goods of eternity. Be confounded to see that they run more swiftly to death than you to life. Think yourselves capable of very little, if a courtier, to gain the favor of an earthly prince, serves him with more fidelity than you serve the king of heaven; and if a soldier, for a shadow of glory and for the wretched share of the spoils which he expects from a battle won, fights against his enemies and struggles with more valor than you do to conquer the world, the devil, and yourselves, and to win by that victory the kingdom of heaven and an immortal glory.[12]

During this long period of his education and his growing apostolate, Ignatius had no clear plan to found a new religious community. As a natural leader, he had gathered groups of young men around him who had had been converted to the service of Christ through the Exercises and who naturally looked to him for direction. In 1534, on the hill of Montmartre in Paris, Ignatius and six of his companions, nearing the

---

[12] Paul Doncouer, S. J., *The Heart of Ignatius* (Baltimore: Helicon Press, 1959), 66.

completion of their studies, made vows together that they would serve Christ in poverty and chastity and would go to Jerusalem and attempt a mission among the Turks. If it did not prove possible to get to the Holy Land (there was intermittent warfare throughout the eastern Mediterranean between the Ottomans and various European powers), they would return to Rome and put themselves at the service of the pope. Six of the seven, including Ignatius, were laymen. There were strong ties of brotherly affection among them but no formal organization. As it happened, they were not able to make the journey to Jerusalem, so after being detained for a time in Venice (where Ignatius was ordained a priest in his forty-sixth year), they made their way to Rome, where they arrived in 1538 and presented themselves to Pope Paul III. It was only at this point that the idea of a new order arose and, despite another wave of fierce attacks against them, in 1540 the pope established the Society of Jesus.

The Third Phase: Ignatius as General

When Ignatius was elected general of the new religious order by his brothers, he flatly refused the office. When a second election was held four days later and he was again elected, he again refused, until his Franciscan confessor told him he needed to stop resisting the Holy Spirit. No doubt some of his resistance was due to his humility, his sense of his unworthiness to rule other men. But there may also have been a subtler factor in play. From the time of his conversion, Ignatius had wanted nothing more than to be a pilgrim on the road with Christ, to call others to love and follow God. He was a missionary at heart, with a burning desire to win for Christ's Kingdom those who were most opposed to it. For him that meant the Turks and the whole Muslim world. He had no special aptitude for organizational detail as that is usually understood; he was the opposite of a bureaucrat, and the fifty years of his life were not an obvious preparation for an administrative post. He may have thought that he would not be good at it. But his brothers saw the nature of his genius more clearly than he did. That genius, the great gift of Ignatius to the Church, was his ability, one could almost call it an instinct, to find the right institutional forms for capturing the work of the Holy Spirit in the new age the Church was encountering.

This gift of incarnating ideals in living forms, so necessary to a flourishing human life, was in operation in Ignatius from the first days of his conversion. Many have found themselves in the midst of a spiritual battle, needing to learn to listen to the voice of God and to turn from the voice of the devil. Ignatius also had such an experience, but he then took matters a crucial step forward: he gathered up what he had learned into a set of rules for the discernment of spirits that he could give to others. Many have battled to attain virtue; Ignatius developed a method for the acquisition of specific virtues. Many have encountered the drama of standing at the crossroads of life and of needing to make a firm choice for the Kingdom; Ignatius distilled his experience of that choice and produced the miracle of the Exercises. By the incarnation of his experience into graced institutional forms, the spiritual wisdom that had been entrusted to him was able to touch the lives of thousands.

To get a sense of the breadth of influence and the impact of the Jesuits, it can help to look at their early growth. At the time of their founding in 1540, there were ten members of the Society. By the year of Ignatius's death in 1556, the number had grown to a thousand, of whom only thirty-five were professed members due to their long training process. By 1580, forty years after their founding, there were five thousand members of the Society in twenty-one provinces. By 1615, at the seventy-five year mark, the Society counted over thirteen thousand members. A time that had been bewailing the ignorance and worldliness of priests was receiving its answer. Highly-trained and devout Jesuit priests were to be found everywhere: preaching and giving retreats, building churches, founding colleges and training young men, establishing missions around the world, providing theological expertise at the Council of Trent, engaging in polemics with Protestants, serving as directors of souls, shedding their blood for the Faith; all in the service of Christ, the Church, and the Holy See. It would not be unreasonable to suggest that the company gathered together under the Jesuit standard during the first 150 years of the order's existence was the most talented, disciplined, and impressively prepared group of men ever assembled for a single cause in the history of the world. When thousands of young men of ability, many from the upper reaches of society, respond with such alacrity to a high and difficult ideal, it is clear that a deep chord has been touched. By a combination of spiritual gift and native genius, Ignatius intuited the needs and aspirations of his time and fathered a form of life that could capture them and apply them across the miles and down the generations.

Ignatius's great task as the first superior and primary inspiration of the new Society of Jesus was to write the Society's Rule, or as it was termed by the Jesuits, their Constitutions. Ignatius knew that he was forming a new instrument for a new time; it was a long and painstaking labor for him. He introduced many innovations into his community.

There was to be no special religious garb. There was to be no obligation to chant Morning and Evening Prayer together in choir. Physical austerities were to be kept to a minimum. The Society would be centrally governed under a superior general, rather than the more traditional form of governance that worked locally by chapter. There was to be no oversight of convents and no female branch of the order. And the training involved for a professed member was to be long and thorough. In a letter to the pope in which Ignatius requested that the Jesuits not be tied down by certain responsibilities, he laid out the ruling idea behind this novel organization: "The other religious orders of the Church's army are like frontline troops drawn up in massive battalions. We are like light armed soldiers ready for sudden battles, going from one side to the other, now here, now there. And for this we must be unencumbered and free from all responsibility of this type."[13] Unencumbered and free for immediate action: with his great capacity for suiting the means to the proper end, Ignatius fashioned his society with this apostolic freedom in mind.

Ignatius's fifteen years as superior general were a kind of living martyrdom. The man who longed to be an itinerant missionary was compelled to live in Rome, chained to a desk, interminably writing thousands of administrative letters as he directed the rapidly increasing activities of the Jesuits around the world. But obedience was at the very heart of his spirituality, and he willingly put to death his personal apostolic inclinations for the sake of the greater glory of God. His missionary desires were not quenched, only channeled in new directions. To the end they would flash out and enkindle others with his burning zeal for the salvation of souls. As he

[13] *Ibid*, 69.

sent young members of the Society to the missions, he would bid them a final farewell: "Go, and set the world on fire!"[14]

Chapter Two

St. Francis Xavier

*"There is no better rest in this restless world
than to face imminent peril
of death solely for the love and service of God our Lord."*

The sixteenth century was a time of change in Europe. There were conflicting developments and striking contrasts such that it is difficult to simply characterize the age. On the one hand, many of Christendom's long-standing social arrangements were tottering, leading some to think that the end of the world was near. On the other, new arrangements and new conceptions of human life were emerging, leading others to speak of the age as a new dawn, a renaissance, filled with exciting new possibilities. Again, Christian Europe was under increasing military threat from a growing Ottoman Empire that was gobbling up territory and curtailing Europe's cultural influence, even posing a threat to its existence. At the same time, the Portuguese were wresting from the Muslims their monopoly on the lucrative spice trade and were opening up the whole of Asia to Europeans, while the Spanish were founding a new empire in the Americas that would turn the Atlantic Ocean from being the limit of the West to an internal European body of water. And again, the Catholic Church, the institution that had carried Europe's spirit for a thousand years, was in severe crisis, in great need of reform, under unprecedented attack, and losing lands and peoples to the new Protestant movements. Yet even as this was happening, fresh and energetic expressions of the Catholic Faith and spirit were springing to life, while new lands and new peoples were entering the Catholic fold, transforming the Church into an international society that stretched across the globe.

According to a myth of the ancient world, the Pillars of Hercules, marking the western end of the Mediterranean Sea at the Strait of Gibraltar, were inscribed with the words *Ne plus ultra*: "Beyond this point, nothing." The words were meant as a warning to mariners that they had reached the limits of the habitable world. The name "mediterranean" meant "in the middle of things," and from Roman times onward the "Roman lake" had marked a significant European boundary, both geographically and imaginatively. But at the turn of the sixteenth century, that self-understanding was undergoing a great change of perspective. With the development of new shipbuilding and navigation techniques producing ships that could brave the waves and winds of the open ocean, the eyes of Europeans were increasingly set on the horizons, east, west, and south. When Charles V became king of Spain in 1516, he changed that ancient warning into a new call for action. He took as his personal motto—adopted as the national motto of Spain—the words *Plus Ultra*: "Further Beyond!" The astonishing missionary adventure of Francis Xavier was among the most compelling examples of this new attitude. Even during his lifetime, and yet more after his death, Xavier came to symbolize for Europe the explosive possibilities of the new age.

Francis Xavier Is Converted to Christ

It was sometimes said of the first two great men of the Jesuit order that Ignatius was the miracle of God, and Xavier was the miracle of Ignatius. A fellow Basque from a similar social background, Francis Xavier had been at the University of Paris for three years before Ignatius arrived, and they became involved with one another almost by accident. Xavier was a young man of strong personality, ardent and forceful emotion, and great charm of personality. He was also aimless and indolent, regularly out of money, and possessed of an unfocused ambition that left him ready to move with the current of life wherever it might take him. He happened to be rooming at the College of Sainte-Barbe with a young Frenchman named Peter Favre when Ignatius came to Paris in 1528 and lodged next door at College Montaigu. Favre was among the first of many students attracted to Ignatius and soon became one of his most fervent disciples. Xavier, on the other hand, wanted nothing to do with the strange and masterful vagabond who had captured his friend's imagination. But he found it impossible to avoid him. When Ignatius completed his Latin studies and was admitted to Sainte-Barbe, he was given lodgings—much to Xavier's disgust—with Favre and himself.

Ignatius took an immediate liking to his fellow country-man, perhaps perceiving what he might become if he were once converted to Christ, and he planned a careful campaign to win Xavier to the cause. It was a long and steady siege, lasting four years, about which we have little information. Ignatius later gave an inkling of what the time had required of him when he commented that Xavier "was the lumpiest dough he had ever kneaded."[1] The crisis point came when Favre was away for an extended period, and Xavier was left to face Ignatius alone. The master angler was rewarded for his patient labor: Xavier took the bait and underwent a powerful conversion. The effect was volcanic. From that point on, during the remaining nineteen years of his life, Xavier would be bound tightly to Ignatius in mind and spirit, bringing all his passion, his strength of will, his immense capacity for hard work, and his chivalric loyalty under the purpose and direction of his friend and spiritual father.

The next seven years after his conversion were for Xavier a time of preparation for a mission he had not yet fully glimpsed, during which he laid the foundations of a deep life of prayer and a pattern of tireless apostolic activity. At this period Xavier's life had the internally devout and externally haphazard quality of the band of men forming around Ignatius. He was one of the seven companions who made vows at Montmartre in 1534. Then late in the next year, with Ignatius off on a visit to Spain, he and his companions set out for Venice traveling overland by foot, taking a roundabout way to avoid a zone of war. According to their vow they would then embark on their proposed mission to the Turks in the Holy Land. They found Ignatius in Venice ahead of them, and while waiting for their plans to ripen, they served in hospitals that had recently been established by Jerome Emiliani and Gaetano da Thiene, both of whom were founders of new religious orders and who would one day be canonized. Xavier was ordained a priest at this time, along with Ignatius and those among the other companions who

---

[1] James Brodrick, S. J., *Saint Francis Xavier* (New York: The Wicklow Press, 1952).

were not yet in orders. Finding the door to the Holy Land closed due to war, the group scattered, converging on Rome to present themselves to the pope.

On the way to Rome, Xavier stopped for some months in Bologna along with Nicholas Bobadilla, another of the companions. It was in Bologna that Xavier's gift and zeal for missionary work began powerfully to show itself. His approach was direct and arresting. He would go to one of the city's crowded piazzas, wave his hat and call to the onlookers to gather their attention, and despite his serious lack of polished Italian, would hold them entranced by his force of personality and the potency of his faith. "After Mass," reported one who witnessed his activity there, "he would spend the entire day hearing confessions, visiting the sick in the hospitals and prisoners in the jails, serving the poor, preaching in the piazzas, and teaching children or other uninstructed persons Christian doctrine."[2] Already at this early stage, Xavier's mind was moving toward the East. "He used to talk frequently and fervently," a priest friend from Bologna remembered, "about the affairs of India and the conversion to our holy faith of its great gentile population. He had his heart set on making the voyage and was all afire to accomplish it before he died."[3]

Xavier traveled to Rome in the spring of 1538, the last of the group of companions to arrive. Now for the first time, the group began to consider together the possibility of establishing themselves as an order. After long discussions far into the night during the spring and summer of 1539, they wrote a short document outlining the structure and aims of their proposed society and presented it to Pope Paul

[2] *Ibid*, 63.
[3] *Ibid*, 76.

III. The idea gained the pope's immediate approval, but due to powerful opposition from other members of the Curia, it was a year before the new order was formally instituted. Before that event came about, Xavier would already have departed from Rome on mission. It is a sign of the impressive depth and clarity of Ignatius's spiritual training that Xavier, who would never again live with Ignatius and his brothers but would be separated from them for many years and by thousands of miles, was so well able to incarnate and express the spirit of the new religious order.

The particular charism or ministry of the new Society, as it was expressed in that first document, was so broad as to include virtually all kinds of priestly ministry. They were to be a community founded "for the advancement of souls in Christian life and doctrine and for the propagation of the faith by the ministry of the word, by spiritual exercises, by works of charity, and expressly by the instruction in Christianity of children and the uneducated." Certain traditional practices usual among religious orders to help maintain unity and cohesion were explicitly absent, notably the duty of praying the Office together. With such a broad scope of apostolate and so little to bind them together in common life, how were they to keep their focus? What was to be their unifying principle? That principle was to be found in the famous "fourth vow" of the Jesuits, obedience to the pope. Here is how the document put the ideal:

> All the companions should know and daily bear in mind, not only when they first make their profession but as long as they live, that this entire Society and each one individually are soldiers of God under faithful obedience to our most holy lord Paul III and his successors and are thus under the command of the Vicar of Christ and his divine power not only as having the obligation to him

which is common to all clerics, but also as being so bound by the bond of a vow that whatever His Holiness commands pertaining to the advancement of souls and the propagation of the faith we must immediately carry out, without any evasion or excuse as far as in us lies, whether he sends us to the Turks or to the New World or to the Lutherans or to others, be they infidel or faithful.[4]

All aspects of the common life were to be subordinated to this readiness for immediate action in whatever direction was necessary under the orders of the pope. This was the "light infantry" model, under the eye of a commanding general, that Ignatius and his brothers placed at the service of the Church.

The men who founded the new Society of Jesus had made a strong impression in Rome and elsewhere, and there were increasing requests for their services. Among the most insistent came from the king of Portugal, whose overseas settlements and colonies were in desperate need of missionaries. Two of the companions had been promised for the Indian mission, neither of them Xavier. But one of the two, Bobadilla, got seriously ill, leaving only one among the companions still free. "Francis," Ignatius said to him, "you know that by order of his Holiness two of us have to go to India, and we chose Bobadilla as one of the two. He cannot go now owing to his illness, nor can the Ambassador wait until he gets better. This is your enterprise." Xavier's response was immediate: "Well, yes! Here I am!"[5] The next day he left with the Portuguese ambassador for Lisbon. He was never to return.

[4] St. Ignatius of Loyola et al., "The First Sketch of the Society of Jesus" in *Catholic Reform: From Cardinal Ximenes to the Council of Trent, 1495–1563,* ed. John C. Olin (New York: Fordham University Press, 1990), 83–4.

[5] Brodrick, *Francis Xavier,* 77–8.

Xavier's Missionary Journeys

Europe had long been isolated from the lands and markets of south and east Asia, due to Muslim control of the trade routes both overland and by sea. During the fifteenth century the Portuguese began to explore ever further afield. Columbus had first sailed westward because he wanted to get to "the Indies." He found instead a huge continent that proved to be its own theater of exploration and settlement, with the lure of silver and gold to make the venture worthwhile. To the east were the ancient and fabled lands of Asia with all their exoticism, their large populations, and their wealth. Of most interest to the European merchants were the spices so coveted in European kitchens. In 1498, the Portuguese mariner Vasco da Gama rounded the southern cape of Africa and arrived in India, bypassing the normal trade routes. In 1510, the city of Goa on India's west coast was conquered by Afonso de Albuquerque, and from there the Portuguese began to stretch out a mercantile empire that gave them access to the markets and materials of the whole of Asia. They established themselves in Malacca in what is now Malaysia, and then went further east to the Moluccas (the famous Spice Islands, now part of Indonesia) and to East Timor and New Guinea. They initiated relations with Thailand and Japan and eventually gained control of the island of Macau off the coast of China. As Xavier was serving under the patronage of the Portuguese crown, his missionary journeys followed the path staked out by the Portuguese.

To understand the great significance of Francis Xavier to his age, it is necessary to catch something of the excitement that was aroused in Europe by the opening up of the globe. Xavier spent only ten years as a missionary in Asia, but those years flamed like a comet above the skies of Europe. In the complex world of western Christendom, the allure of glory, gold, and immortal souls for Christ were smelted together in an alloy that we now find difficult to comprehend. Europe followed Xavier's missionary exploits through the letters he sent to his Jesuit brothers, some of which they circulated and published. Though he hardly knew it and would not have cared about it, Xavier was a famous man in Europe before he died. He seemed to be accomplishing on a spiritual plane the sort of conquests that other explorers and conquistadors were gaining in more worldly terms.

To briefly set out Xavier's missionary itinerary gives some sense of his remarkable labors. He set sail from Lisbon in 1541. Rounding the Cape of Good Hope, he put in at Mozambique on the southeast coast of Africa, where he worked among the locals for six months while he waited for favorable winds. He arrived at the Indian port city of Goa in the spring of 1542. After four months there, he traveled south to Cochin on the southern coast of India and spent more than a year as a lone missionary among the pearl-diving population. He then returned to Goa for some months and returned to Cochin for another year. In 1545 he took ship for Malacca in Malaysia. By this time he had become well known, and people there were awaiting him. In early 1546, he left Malacca and journeyed east to the Moluccas and the people of the Spice Islands. The next year he returned to Malacca, where he remained for another six months. He then journeyed back to Goa, visiting along the way all the groups among whom he had established missions. He then spent more than a year in Goa, where among other duties he attended to the growing Jesuit mission—by 1548 there were seventeen Jesuits in India. In

1549 he headed back east, arriving in Japan, where he opened a mission and stayed for two years. He then returned again to Goa. In 1552 he set out from Goa one last time, hoping to gain access to China. In December of that year, Francis Xavier died on the island of Shangchuan, waiting for a boat that would take him to the Chinese mainland.

The distance covered in all this travel is staggering. Xavier voyaged tens of thousands of miles by ship, at a time when it was not rare for half of the passengers to die on any given voyage. He walked many hundreds of miles, going from village to village among the peoples he was serving. He faced constant exposure to heat and storms, and was regularly sick with unnamed tropical diseases. Beyond his travels, he kept up a regimen of extraordinary missionary activity. He slept only two or three hours a night, spending the remaining hours in prayer. He ate little, paying no attention to his physical health. He preached and taught incessantly. According to best estimates, he baptized something like thirty thousand people. He heard confessions by the thousands, visited and anointed the sick, said masses for lepers, and presided at burials. He wrote songs for children and the illiterate with lyrics taken from the words of the Creed. Never a particularly brilliant student, he spent long tedious hours attempting to learn something of the languages of the various peoples among whom he served. He organized the mission work of the other Jesuits in his care.

One of his longtime associates who had known him in Portugal and in the Indian mission remembered his extraordinary energy:

> No human being could have done what he did or have lived as he lived without being full of the Holy Spirit. ...If he could

find time in the night, as he never could during the day, he gave himself completely to prayer and contemplation. Day and night, he consoled men, hearing their confessions, visiting them when sick, begging alms for them when they were poor. He had nothing of his own, and on himself never spent a penny. As much as one could dream of a man doing he did, and more.[6]

No wonder stories and legends sprouted around him like flowers. Those who watched his indefatigable activity and his unrelenting zeal were not surprised that Xavier died after a seemingly short ten years of mission; they were amazed that he lasted half that time.

Xavier's Missionary Principles

Goa, Xavier's first Indian destination, was an immense and bustling city, many times as large as Rome or London. When he first landed there, Xavier was nearly overwhelmed by his sense of his own inadequacies. Soon after arriving he wrote to his brothers: "In God's name and for His glory, tell me fully and clearly what ought to be my method of approach to the pagans and Moors of the country to which I am now going. It is my hope that by means of you God will teach me how I must proceed in order to convert them to His holy faith. Your letters will show me the blunders to avoid, the wrong methods which I must change." He was also sobered by the great missionary need. "Dust and ashes as I am, and made to feel still more puny and despicable by witnessing with my own eyes the need of priests out here, I would be forever the slave of all who had the heart to come and labor in this vast vineyard of the Lord."[7]

[6] *Ibid*, 252.
[7] *Ibid*, 128–9.

But Xavier was never one to moon over difficulties. His natural energetic optimism, deepened and purified by an intense confidence in God, soon saw him up and active. Here is how one of his missionary associates described his approach to bringing the Gospel to the Goans:

> He went up and down the streets and squares with a bell in his hand, crying to the children and others to come to the instructions. The novelty of the proceeding, never seen before in Goa, brought a large crowd around him which he then led to the church. He began by singing the lessons which he had rhymed and then made the children sing them so that they might become the better fixed in their memories. Afterwards he explained each point in the simplest way, using only such words as his young audience could readily understand. By this method, which has since been adopted everywhere in the Indies, he so deeply engrained the truths and precepts of the faith in the hearts of the people that men and women, children and old folk, took to singing the Ten Commandments while they walked the streets, as did the fisherman in his boat and the laborers in the fields, for their own entertainment and recreation.[8]

Francis was a great heart rather than a profound analytical thinker; but his intuitive capacity for reaching people helped him to pioneer methods of evangelization that put an emphasis on finding points of contact between the Gospel and the local culture. He would then build his missionary enterprise around those areas of understanding, an approach that has since come to be called missionary enculturation. Xavier's instinctive sense of the principle of enculturation can be seen in his dealings with the Japanese. In India, and later in Malaysia and Indonesia, Xavier worked largely among the

[8] *Ibid*, 120.

poorest and least educated classes, adapting his method to their abilities. In coming to Japan, Xavier recognized that he was dealing with a highly sophisticated and well-educated populace. He abandoned his earlier method, giving more attention to the forms of Japanese life: manners of politeness, care in dress, and delicacy of communication. He knew that waving his hat and ringing a bell in the town square was no way to win a hearing for the Gospel among the Japanese. The point may seem obvious to us, but it was revolutionary in its time. Some years later the missionary principles pioneered by Xavier would be developed in a more systematic way by his successors in the Jesuit mission to Asia, Alessandro Valignano and Matteo Ricci.

The most powerful principle at work in Xavier's missionary activity, if it can be called a principle, was his evident love for those he was evangelizing. He genuinely cared for the people among whom he worked, and his warm-hearted concern for them broke down every barrier of language and culture. In this Xavier transcended his age. According to the biases of his birth and background, Xavier should have had every reason for despising these people. They were uneducated, poor, and, worst of all, pagan. Many Europeans of his time would have viewed them as little more than animals. But not Xavier. He wrote to one of his fellow missionaries: "I entreat you to bear yourself very lovingly towards those people. Learn to pardon and support their weaknesses very patiently, reflecting that if they are not good now, they will be some day."[9] He fought against the typical attitude of disdain among the Portuguese for the native populations among whom they lived. To young Jesuit recruits who were just coming to the mission, he wrote:

[9] *Ibid*, 167.

"Be careful never to criticize the native Christians in the presence of the Portuguese. Rather must you take their part and speak up in their defense, for they have been so short a time Christians and have so small a grasp of the faith that the Portuguese ought to be surprised to find them as good as they are. Try with all your might, Fathers, to win the love of your people, doing whatever you do for them with words of love."[10] He had a special delight for the Japanese: "They are the best race yet discovered," he wrote, "and I think that among non-Christians their match will not easily be found."[11]

It was the strength of this heart of love, a reflection of the heart of Christ, that made Xavier so eager to win recruits to the mission. Two years after his arrival in India, he wrote a letter to his Jesuit brothers that was widely circulated and that created a storm in Europe, inspiring many young men to sign up for missionary work.

> Multitudes out here fail to become Christians only because there is nobody prepared for the holy task of instructing them. I have often felt strongly moved to descend on the universities of Europe, especially Paris and its Sorbonne, and to cry aloud like a madman to those who have more learning than good will to employ it advantageously, telling them how many souls miss Heaven and fall into Hell through their negligence! I fear many university men pursue their studies and conform to regulations purely in order to attain to dignities, benefices, bishoprics, which gained, they say, it will be time enough to serve God. ... What multitudes of gentiles would become Christians if only there were priests to help them! ... Out here, people flock into the Church in such numbers that my arms are often almost paralyzed with baptizing, and my voice gives out completely through

[10] *Ibid*, 312.
[11] *Ibid*, 361.

repeating endlessly in their tongue the Creed, the commandments, and the prayers.[12]

Xavier's love for those he was evangelizing could provoke a stern reproof from him toward the Portuguese who maltreated them and gave a poor example of the Christian Faith. He regularly chided government officials who turned their eyes from illegal and unjust practices for the sake of personal gain. Six years into his mission he wrote a letter to King John of Portugal, who was interested in the spread of the Faith and had originally sought Jesuits for the Indian mission. Xavier was angry about the depredations of his appointed governors:

> Should he [the governor in question] neglect to carry out your Highness's intentions of greatly promoting the growth of our holy Faith, assure him that you are determined to punish him and tell him with a solemn oath that, when he returns to Portugal, you will declare all his property forfeit, and besides put him in irons for several years. ... If the Governor is brought to understand that you certainly mean what you say, the whole island of Ceylon will be Christian in a year, and so also will be many kings, as those of Malabar, Cape Comorin, and several other places.[13]

But if not, "your Highness need not count on any increase of our holy Faith nor on the perseverance of those at present Christians, no matter how many appointments and dispositions you make."[14] A bold letter to send to a king.

Xavier's love for his people was more than repaid in their love for him. His engaging personality and his tireless service won their hearts and drew them to him. Whenever he was about

---

[12] *Ibid*, 157–8.
[13] *Ibid*, 306–7.
[14] *Ibid*.

to leave one of the missions, the people would gather around him and beg him to stay. Xavier wrote of one such experience, "When the time came to leave, I embarked about midnight so as to avoid the weeping and mourning of my devoted friends, men and women. But my friends found me out and I could not hide from them. The night and the parting from these my spiritual sons and daughters helped me to feel my unworthiness."[15] A Japanese man who had first sought Xavier out about the possibility of coming to his people said of him: "I would lay down my life a hundred times for the love I bear him."[16]

Xavier's Last Journey

Xavier had been in the Indian mission for ten years, and away from Rome for twelve, when Ignatius, his friend and superior, thought the time had come for him to return to Europe. No doubt Ignatius would delight in seeing him again, but more to the point was his conviction that Xavier could do more than anyone else to speak to European authorities about the needs and possibilities of the overseas missions. He therefore sent him the directive: "Looking always to the greater service of God and the help of souls in those parts and considering how much their good depends on Portugal, I have determined to order you in virtue of holy obedience to take the first opportunity of a good passage to Portugal, in the name of Christ our Lord."[17] But by the time the letter arrived in Goa, Francis had been dead for seven months.

During his time in Japan, Xavier had heard about China. He knew nothing of its language and little of its customs; but

[15] *Ibid*, 283.
[16] *Ibid*, 312.
[17] *Ibid*, 464.

he knew that it was a large and civilized country, ruled by law, and highly respected by the Japanese. With that little bit of knowledge, but with a great desire to spread the Gospel, he set out to conquer the Middle Kingdom for Christ. "I am in great hope," he wrote to Ignatius, "that by the labors of the Society of Jesus both Chinese and Japanese will abandon their idolatries and adore God and Jesus Christ."[18] He took four men with him. The prospects of their getting into China were not high, but Xavier was not easily daunted. They made their long way from Goa to the island of Shangchuan, not far from Canton. There they waited, Xavier looking out day after day upon the sea for the merchant vessel that would take them across to the mainland. The promised ship never came, and Xavier took ill. After a few weeks of sickness, the seemingly unstoppable dynamo of missionary energy died a quiet death, calling on the names of Jesus and Mary.

There might seem something akin to the hopeless exploits of Cervantes's Don Quixote in Xavier's attempt to master the Chinese Empire in such a fashion. But his unlikely missionary initiative toward that great civilization can better be read in the realm of the Spirit than by its immediate practical possibilities. The Jesuit who did eventually found a Chinese mission, Matteo Ricci, noted Xavier's achievement: "All the Blessed Father's stratagems for entering China fell to the ground, but we may well believe that if he could not obtain from God the privilege for himself, he obtained it in Heaven for us his companions who, against all human hope, succeeded when he was thirty years dead."[19]

Xavier's remains slowly made their way back to Goa. When his body finally reached the city, there was a spontaneous

[18] *Ibid*, 492.
[19] *Ibid*, 520.

upsurge of emotion. Bells rang, thousands of people gathered, and the whole city was stirred to its depths. For four days crowds thronged into the church where the great missionary lay, for the chance to touch or kiss the body, which, though almost a year dead, was un-decayed and fresh. A year and a half later, the body was exhumed and attested by an attending physician to be both un-embalmed and still preserved. A century and a half later the shrine was opened yet again, and the body was found still to be in a remarkable state of preservation. Like his body, Xavier's memory has remained fresh. And though he was never able to return to Rome, his right hand and forearm, the one with which he performed so many baptisms, was brought back to the Church of the Gesù, where it lies in close proximity to Loyola's remains. There is a fittingness in this final union of the two friends. Ignatius had kneaded more of his own missionary spirit into that lumpy dough of Francis Xavier than into any other, and Xavier had carried that spirit with him, united to his own indomitable will and deep faith, even to the ends of the earth.

Chapter Three

St. Teresa of Ávila

"Solo Dios basta."

Wherever the Kingdom of God is preached and lived, there will be some among the faithful called to a life of consecrated contemplation. The scriptural figures of Elijah and John the Baptist in the desert, Simeon and Anna praying in the Temple of Jerusalem, and Mary the sister of Martha and Lazarus sitting at the feet of Christ have resonated down the centuries as examples of an essential expression of Christian discipleship. "We look not to the things that are seen," wrote St. Paul, "but to the things that are unseen; for the things that are seen are transient, but the things that are unseen are eternal" (2 Cor 4:18). According to the vision of reality given by Christ, the whole of the seen world is a kind of outward clothing that rests upon invisible realities, and the real business of life is to use the seen things to approach the more important and lasting unseen world. This being so, it makes sense that Jesus would defend Mary from the complaints of her sister Martha and insist that in setting her gaze upon him, Mary had chosen "the good portion," the one thing necessary (cf. Lk 10:41).

Through the long centuries of Christianity, from the explosion of the monastic movement in fourth-century Egypt to the crystallization of the contemplative spirit in religious communities of many places and times, contemplative men and women have played a role of importance in the Church's life out of all proportion to their numbers. They have been a kind of spiritual heart, a vital organ of Christ's Body that has held the whole Christian people in proper relation to eternal realities. Through their intercessory prayer, their battling with demonic forces, their lifting a constant song of praise to Heaven, their keeping a vision of the invisible world clear and present, and their incarnating in time the Christian hope of eternity, the often hidden lives of contemplatives have gained for the Church much of her spiritual potency. As the contemplative goes, so goes the Church as a whole. It is therefore not surprising to find that a great deal of spiritual conflict swirls around these congregations.

The attack on contemplative life comes from two main directions. The first of these is a frontal assault on the very idea of a life given entirely to prayer and solitude. Because the contemplative life makes no sense whatever apart from the existence of an invisible world, it is a standing challenge to worldliness. For the person with no faith, it can hardly seem anything but mentally imbalanced to spend all of one's time on what are considered only phantoms. Contemplatives have been called antisocial, drawing off otherwise useful members of the society into idleness and self-absorption, breaking up families, and walling up healthy young men and women in a fruitless existence. At the very least they have been thought foolish, wasting their time on unimportant matters while the great world passes them by. It was not for nothing that the French revolutionary armies destroyed every monastery they could find or that Napoleon forcibly dissolved any religious order that could not demonstrate its immediate social utility. For those who were aggressively pursuing a vision of the world that began and ended with what was seen, it was necessary to destroy the cultural and spiritual influence of those monuments to the unseen world. But even for believers, Mary's "good portion" can present a problem. Contemplatives have been accused by other Christians of cowardice in attempting to escape the hard realities of the world and have been berated for laziness in shirking Christian responsibilities of evangelizing and serving the needy. Jesus's defense of Mary has been a needed corrective in every age.

A second attack on contemplative life comes in a subtler form and arises from a happier and more natural, but not less debilitating, process. An old saying has it that the contemplative leaves the world, and then the world seeks out the contemplative. Again and again the pattern has repeated itself: an individual or a group of men or women have left normal society and have pursued solitude and poverty to follow the contemplative vocation. Like Anthony, they have penetrated the inhospitable desert or, like Benedict, have sought out lonely mountain caves. They have gone deep into the dark and untamed forests like Bruno and Bernard or, more strangely, have settled themselves on platforms high in the midst of the city like Simeon Stylites.

But wherever they have gone, however much they have attempted to flee the world, the world has followed them. Much to their surprise, contemplatives have regularly found themselves important members of their societies, surrounded by the trappings of usefulness and even of power and wealth. St. Benedict has been called the father of European civilization and not without good reason; but founding or saving a civilization was nowhere on the list of his intended achievements. It all seems to happen innocently enough, even by a kind of accident: the innate strength of a life focused on the worship of God and the mastery of the self spills over into all manner of social benefits.

But this integration of the contemplative into normal social life brings with it a creeping worldliness. The great danger for a house of contemplation is not that it will become a den of iniquity; despite the fog of the Black Legend, few monasteries or convents in history have been places of obvious evil. When contemplative life gets corrupted, monks and nuns do not typically become criminals. Their problem, one that is often more difficult to address, is that they grow comfortable. Rather than maintaining their true nature as outposts of vigilant prayer, frontline fortresses against the powers of darkness, strongholds of solitude preserving the fundamentally otherworldly nature of the Church by their worship and their witness, they lapse into pleasant lodgings for the spiritually inclined to enjoy a life of relative ease.

In 1662, in the city of Ávila in Spain, a handful of nuns of the Carmelite order began a new foundation under the protection of St. Joseph. Their prioress was the forty-seven-year-old Teresa Sánchez de Cepeda y Ahumada. The founding would prove to be a significant event in the reform of the Church's contemplative life and therefore of great importance for the life of the Church as a whole. And in the character and writings of Teresa of Ávila, the Church was given a remarkable personality and a source of spiritual vitality that has reached far beyond the world of Carmel.

Teresa is a highly attractive figure. She has been one of Spain's favorite saints. It says something of her popularity that she has been proposed as patron of her country, which would mean displacing the great Santiago, the Apostle James. Her autobiography has been the most widely read book in Spain after Cervantes's *Don Quixote*. Her works on prayer are spiritual classics, and in 1970 she was declared by Pope Paul VI a Doctor of the Church, the first woman ever to have been given that honor. But if she has been attractive to moderns, she has also been difficult to understand. An age that has lost sympathy with its ancestors and that has little understanding of traditional faith can find in Teresa a bundle of contradictions. She is such an irrepressible personality, so full of warmth and honesty, and so obviously strong and courageous, that we want her to be one of us. But how could such a talented woman have desired to shut herself up in a convent? How could such a strong-minded individual have lived so willingly under the authority of the Church and of the crown in an age when the Spanish Inquisition was at its most active? So we find ways to adjust the seeming paradox. She was an irreverent proto-feminist; she was a politically clever operator who knew how to feign obedience in order to make her way in an authoritarian world; and perhaps most persistently, she was able, despite her Catholic faith and her profession as a Carmelite nun, to be "her own person." But the glory of St. Teresa is precisely that she expended all of her energies of mind and will to make sure that she was not her own person. With all the considerable force of her being, she wanted to belong to another. She is a shining example of the truth taught by Christ that we find perfect freedom in perfect obedience, that we grow larger when we make ourselves smaller, and that we most find ourselves in all the particularities of our personalities exactly when we most lose ourselves in God.

Teresa's Early Life and Conversion

Teresa was born in 1515 in the Ávila region of Spain, the sixth of twelve children. Her father was a wealthy merchant who had bought a knighthood. Her mother was from a family of high Spanish nobility. Her grandfather on her father's side was Jewish and had been degraded as a *converso*, one who had become Catholic but who had been found by the Inquisition to be continuing some aspect of Jewish practice or belief. But this taint in the family's noble lineage had been hushed up and forgotten. The home in which Teresa grew up was comfortable and devout. From a young age it was clear that Teresa had strong gifts of personality. She was outgoing and attractive, and she knew how to please those around her. She was a natural leader among her friends and her siblings.

The first serious shock in Teresa's life came in her fourteenth year when her mother, to whom she was deeply attached, died. Two years later she was sent to a convent school, but it was not long before the ill health that would dog her throughout her life forced her to return home. At the age of twenty, she slipped away without telling her father and joined the Carmelite Convent of the Incarnation, a well-established house in Ávila with some 150 nuns in residence. Her decision to enter religious life was sincere but not particularly passionate. It seemed to be something of a marriage of convenience. She had no doubt about the truths of the Catholic Faith, and she wanted to gain salvation. She thought that entrance into a convent was the safest way to gain that end. In this she was similar to many of her contemporaries in religious communities.

Teresa begins her autobiography with the following injunction to the reader:

> I beg anyone who reads this account to bear in mind, for the love of the Lord, how wicked my life has been—so wicked, indeed, that among all the Saints who have turned to God I can find none whose history affords me any comfort. For I see that, once the Lord called them, they never fell back into sin. I, however, not only fell back and became worse, but seem deliberately to have sought ways of resisting the favors which His Majesty granted me.[1]

These strong words, repeated in different ways throughout Teresa's account, might seem to point to a past that had been filled with the worst sort of iniquity. But there was never a time in Teresa's life, from her girlhood on, when she was not a believing Christian, saying her prayers, avoiding serious sin, and living under the shadow of the Church's teachings. She was not a Magdalene, an Augustine, or an Ignatius— someone who came to faith after wandering far from God. Yet when she writes this way she is not merely affecting a pose or tossing off pious phrases; the evident honesty of her self-assessment rules out that possibility. What could she have meant by accusing herself of such wickedness?

Some have seen in Teresa's self-condemnation the expression of a wounded spirit that had been crushed by the overly strict demands of a disciplinarian father and further oppressed by her experience as a woman and as a person with Jewish blood in sixteenth-century Spain. To put it in modern therapeutic terms, she denigrated herself because she was someone with low self-esteem who saw herself in an inaccurately negative light. The difficulty with this reading is that there is virtually nothing in Teresa's manner of going through life that showed this kind of wound. She had all the

---

[1] Teresa of Ávila, *The Life of St. Teresa of Ávila*, J. M. Cohen, trans. (London: Penguin Books, 1957), 21.

confidence and self-assurance of her Spanish noble upbringing, an attitude of bold decisiveness that was often described as masculine, combined with a commonsensical insight into others that allowed her to view the world with an ironically humorous lens. She had a generous measure of courage and resilience in all her dealings with the world. Her sense of her own wickedness was not in any observable way a psychological symptom. Its source was elsewhere.

Teresa is not alone in this saintly habit of self-condemnation. It is also notably present in Francis of Assisi and Philip Neri, two of the most joyful personalities known to history. Paradoxically, their joy in life and their dismay at their own darkness come from the same source: a profound insertion into the being of God. Those who are closest to God see most clearly his love and mercy; they also see more clearly than others the horror of a will that turns from him. So with Teresa—the sins she saw in herself were not the stuff of tabloids. But where great light is given and great love is present, even a seemingly small offense becomes a serious matter.

In any case, as Teresa lays out her inner life, she notes that soon after her entry into the convent, during a protracted period of grave illness, she was given the grace of prayer and union with God, but she then turned from that grace and for many years avoided praying. During this time she lived outwardly as a model Carmelite according to the customs of the day—she was faithful to the communal prayers and lived an ordered life—but she was not regularly practicing meditative, or mental, prayer. As a result, she began to lose pleasure in the life of virtue. "I was vain," she writes, "and knew how to get credit for those qualities usually esteemed in the world."[2] Because she did many things that gave the appearance of virtue, she was given a wide latitude in receiving visitors and in leaving the house to make visits to others. "Though my follies were sometimes crystal clear, they [the sisters] would not believe them since they always thought much of me."[3] She described the general tenor of her life as outwardly respectable but inwardly miserable:

> I spent nearly twenty years on this stormy sea, falling and evermore rising again, but to little purpose as afterwards I would fall once more. My life was so far from perfection that I took hardly any notice of venial sins, and, though I feared mortal sins, I was not sufficiently afraid to keep myself out of temptations. I derived no joy from God and no pleasure from the world.[4]

She called her experience "one of the most painful ways of life that can be imagined."[5] A convent may be a place of refuge from external distractions and battles, but that outward protection only brings the inner battles of the soul more clearly into focus. Those interior struggles, when honestly faced, can be the most difficult to manage. And Teresa was nothing if not honest.

But through this period of misery, God was preparing something extraordinary for her. At a certain point her desire for meditative prayer began to grow again, and she experienced a new grace and ease in its practice. The turning point came when she happened upon a statue of Christ in agony that had been brought into the convent for the celebration of a festival. Touched by the grace of God, she saw the sufferings

---

2 *Ibid*, 42.
3 *Ibid*, 51.
4 *Ibid*, 56.
5 *Ibid*, 61.

of Christ in a new light and was overcome by remorse for the weakness of her response. She was transfixed, and she stayed before the statue weeping until she was sure that her prayers for a deeper life in Christ had been answered. She was given the grace to make the final offering of herself, to hold nothing back, to become, as she would later say, a servant of love. She often called this experience her second, and deeper, conversion. The change is noted dramatically in her autobiography:

> From now onwards this is a new book—I mean another and new life. Up to now the life I described was my own. But the life I have been living since I began to expound these methods of prayer is one which God has been living in me—or so it has seemed to me.[6]

Teresa's "second conversion" took place in her fortieth year, in 1555. She was greatly helped along the way by the reforming Franciscan friar Peter of Alcántara and by the Jesuits who had recently been established in Spain, notably Francis Borgia, who was for a time her confessor. During the next five years, she experienced a spiritual revolution. She lost interest in the social visits that she had earlier found so attractive and plunged ever more deeply into prayer. She received many graces of contemplation in the form of visions and locutions and often was drawn into the quiet prayer of union with God. It was during this time that she had the experience, famously captured by Bernini's sculpture at the Church of Maria della Vittoria in Rome, of being painfully pierced by the love of God. She writes:

> Beside me, on the left hand, appeared an angel in bodily form. He was not tall, but short, and very beautiful. In his hands I saw a great golden spear, and at the iron tip there appeared to be a point of fire.

[6] *Ibid*, 162.

This he plunged into my heart several times so that it penetrated to my entrails. When he pulled it out, I felt that he took them with it, and left me utterly consumed by the great love of God. The pain was so severe that it made me utter several moans. The sweetness caused by this intense pain is so extreme that one cannot possibly wish it to cease, nor is one's soul then content with anything but God. This is not a physical, but a spiritual pain. ... So gentle is this wooing which takes place between God and the soul.[7]

During this five-year period, Teresa was schooled in the ways of contemplative prayer that would form the content of her books of spiritual teaching.

Teresa's immersion in the life of God brought her face to face with a Christian paradox that has pervaded the lives of many of the saints. Jesus said to his disciples, "You shall love the Lord your God with all your heart, and with all your soul, and with all your mind, and with all your strength" (Mk 12:30). He also said, "I will warn you whom to fear: fear him who, after he has killed, has power to cast into hell; yes, I tell you, fear him!" (Lk 12:5). For many, love and fear are mutually exclusive dispositions. We think that we cannot love what we fear and that we do not fear what we love. In Teresa, her deeper conversion meant the integration of her response to the presence of God at a higher level. She experienced both her love and her fear of God growing apace with each other.

As to love of God: Teresa's warm heart constantly overflowed with expressions of her delight at the love and mercy of her Beloved.

O my God, how infinitely good you are! O joy of the angels, when I think of it, I long to dissolve in love for you! How true it is that you suffer those who will not suffer you to be with them! What a good

---

[7] *Ibid*, 210.

friend you are, O my Lord, to comfort and endure them, and wait for them to rise to your condition, and yet in the meantime to be patient of the state they are in! You take into account, O Lord, the times they loved you, and for one moment of penitence you forget all their offences against you.[8]

The whole of Teresa's life was an extended act of love offered to the God who meant everything to her.

As to fear of God: Teresa recorded a vision she received in which she was shown the place the devil had prepared for her in Hell. It was deeply troubling to her: "I was terrified, and though this happened six years ago, I am still terrified as I write; even as I sit here my natural heat seems to be drained away by fear." Yet she understood this horrific experience to be motivated by, and to give depth to, her love. "This vision was one of the greatest mercies that the Lord had bestowed on me. It has benefited me very much, both by freeing me from fear of the tribulations and oppositions of this life, and by giving me the strength, while bearing them, to give thanks to the Lord, who, as I now believe, has delivered me from these continuous and terrible torments."[9]

Teresa's Missionary Foundations

The origins of the Carmelite order are lost in a haze of uncertain history and golden legend. Early traditions within the order held that it was begun by the prophet Elijah. By all accounts, the Blessed Mother had a decisive hand in the inspiration of its founding; the official name of the male order is "the Order of the Brothers of the Blessed Virgin Mary of Mount Carmel." The site of Mount Carmel in Israel

[8] *Ibid*, 63.
[9] *Ibid*, 234.

seems traditionally to have been a favored place for hermits. In 1185, a group of monks were found to be living there, and they were given a rule by the Latin patriarch of the crusader kingdom Jerusalem. This event marks the official beginning of the Carmelites as a Catholic order. Increasing danger from Saracens and tension between the eastern and western Churches motivated the order to relocate to Europe around 1242. In 1245, under the patronage of Pope Innocent IV, they adopted a rule more suited to European conditions. No longer classified as monks, they took their place alongside the three existing mendicant orders (Franciscans, Dominicans, and Augustinians), which meant, among other provisions, that they were not required to work, but could subsist on alms. Like the other mendicant orders, the Carmelites grew rapidly and spread throughout Europe. Then in 1432, in what came to be a point of contention, Pope Eugenius IV allowed the order a different rule that relaxed much of their earlier austerity. This new set of constitutions came to be called the mitigated rule. The Convent of the Incarnation in Ávila that Teresa joined was conducted under the discipline of this rule.

Teresa's deeper conversion sparked in her a growing desire to live under a stricter rule of life, one that included more time for contemplation, more asceticism and penitential exercises, and greater seclusion from the world. She longed for the earlier expression of the Carmelite charism, and she came to think that the order needed to be reformed in a stricter direction. Her desire was fueled by a vision she received of St. Joseph, encouraging her to found a new house. In 1562, her hopes were realized with the establishment of the Convent of St. Joseph in Ávila. Teresa wrote the constitutions for the new house, basing them on the earlier Carmelite rule. She made habits out of coarse material for the four sisters who joined her in the undertaking. The new reform came to be called the Discalced (barefoot) Carmelites; and though the sisters seldom went without shoes, they took for themselves the rough peasant sandal typical of the time as a sign of their chosen poverty. Teresa originally proposed to limit the number of nuns to twelve to keep the convent from becoming too comfortable or powerful. She wrote of the new foundation, "Their joy was in being alone, and they assured me they were never long enough alone; and so they looked on it as a torment whenever anyone came to see them, even though it were a brother. She who had the most opportunities of being alone in a hermitage considered herself the happiest."[10]

The new Convent of St. Joseph was a modest enough venture. But it set off a storm of struggle and controversy in Ávila so great that the priest serving as chaplain said that it was as though the city had been attacked simultaneously by fire, plague, and an invading army. "I was astonished," wrote Teresa, "at all the trouble the devil was taking about a few poor women, and at the universal belief that a mere dozen sisters and a Prioress would do such harm to the town while living so strictly."[11] We might ask, why all this tumult? Why such harsh opposition to what was a praiseworthy initiative, or at least a harmless one? To understand the sharp antagonism to Teresa and her reform is to open a window on a different kind of society, one that took spiritual matters very seriously, believing them to have profound practical implications. The Spain of Teresa's day had a hundred thousand men and

---

[10] Teresa of Ávila, *The Book of the Foundations of St. Teresa of Jesus* (London: Aeterna Press, 2015), 54.

[11] Teresa of Ávila, *Autobiography*, 272.

women in religious orders. Those religious communities were at the center of Spanish life, and a significant development among them was felt at all levels of the society, from the king to the peasantry.

The opposition to Teresa's new foundation came from various quarters and for different reasons. First, there was an implied critique of existing Carmelite life in the very notion of a needed reform. Many among the Carmelites were resentful at this accusatory finger. "I was very unpopular throughout the convent for wanting to found a more strictly enclosed house," Teresa wrote. "The nuns said that this was an insult to them; that I could serve God just as well where I was, since there were others there better than myself; that I had no love for my own house, and that I should have been better employed raising money for it than for founding another. Some said that I ought to be put in the prison-cell."[12] A second set of concerns came from certain theologians of the Inquisition. Teresa was known to have been the recipient of mystical graces, and those responsible for the discipline of the Church were concerned at the potentially explosive ramifications of visionary experiences. The Protestant Reformation had roiled through western Christendom and had torn many European states apart, often at the hands of prophetic claims to special revelation. There were also "illuminati" in Spain who were claiming that their mystical connection with God did away with their need for a Church or for the sacramental life. At such a time, it was understandable, if not commendable, to find Church authorities overly careful about mystical movements, thinking that it was better to be safe even at the risk of quashing genuine inspiration. This risk-averse attitude meant

[12] *Ibid*, 242.

that for many in authority, any claim to mystical experience was immediately under suspicion. Yet a third set of concerns came from Teresa's insistence that the new foundation was not to be endowed, lest the sisters be unable to practice true poverty. The bishop of Ávila and many of the townspeople were opposed to the establishment of yet another religious house that would need to be supported by the alms of the residents of the city; and other religious orders whose livelihood came from collecting alms were not pleased at the appearance of a competitor for possible funds.

Nonetheless, despite formidable opposition, the house was established, thanks to Teresa's combination of fervent faith, winning personality, and ability to manage practical affairs. With the founding of St. Joseph's Convent, Teresa took the name Teresa of Jesus; she was now close to fifty years old, and she thought that she had found a place of prayer and seclusion where she might live out the rest of her days in relative peace. "As I am now out of the world," she wrote toward the end of her autobiography, "and in a small and saintly society, I look down on things as from a height and care very little what people say or know about me. It seems that the Lord has at last been pleased to bring me to a haven, which I trust in His Majesty will be secure."[13] But it was not to be.

Four years after the founding of the new convent, the general of the Carmelites paid an unprecedented visit to Spain and arrived in the city of Ávila. Teresa was afraid that the general might take offense at the new Discalced convent since it had been founded under the protection of the local bishop rather than under Carmelite authority. She met with him

[13] *Ibid*, 313.

and opened her heart concerning her hopes for a reformed Carmelite house, recounting the ways the convent had been blessed since its opening. The general, who was himself concerned for reform, was deeply moved by what he saw, and not only did he approve the foundation, but he encouraged her to make as many more foundations as she could. Pius V had come to the papal office the year before, and a new wind of reform was blowing through the Church. Thus began for Teresa a fifteen-year period of intense activity, ending only with her death, during which time she founded sixteen more convents of the Discalced Carmelites in locations all over Spain and supported the founding of as many houses of friars. She was helped in this project by, among others, St. John of the Cross, whom she had won as a young priest to the cause of Carmelite reform. There would be many battles to face; the Discalced Carmelites would have a stormy time before they were finally given status as a congregation in their own right. But that first foundation of St. Joseph's, begun with a few sisters, was the spiritual wedge that broke open the field for a fertile harvest.

Nothing shows Teresa's ability to lead others and to manage practical affairs better than her term as prioress of her own Convent of the Incarnation in Ávila. This was the house where she had lived for more than twenty years before leaving it to establish the Convent of St. Joseph under the reformed rule. Now ten years had passed, and Teresa's reform was growing: between 1567 and 1571 she had established eight new Discalced convents and was busily looking after them. The Carmelite provincial, no friend to the reform, wanted to curtail Teresa's activity; he was also concerned at the growing laxity and administrative chaos at Ávila's large convent. So he decided to take care of both matters at once by appointing Teresa as the new prioress. Teresa characteristically obeyed, leaving the future of the reform in God's hands. The effect in Ávila of Teresa's appointment was cataclysmic. It had always been the custom for members of the convent to elect their own superior. To have one thrust upon them in this manner was hard enough, but to have that one be the same Teresa who had thrown the convent and the city into such turmoil ten years previously was not to be borne. As Teresa walked in solemn procession with the provincial to take up her new duties, she was harassed and insulted by the townspeople. When the procession arrived at the convent, they found it barricaded against them. After forcing his way in, the provincial installed Teresa amid screams and shouts from the outraged nuns. A less propitious beginning to a term of office could hardly be imagined.

Yet Teresa's three-year term was a distinct success. Her first act in gathering the mutinous sisters together was to place a statue of the Blessed Mother in the chair of the prioress, so as to make clear who was the true head of the house. She told the sisters that she understood their position and that she would not force upon them the more rigorous practices of the reform. She brought order to the house's finances, which meant that for the first time in many months the sisters had enough to eat. She engaged John of the Cross as spiritual director, a ministry for which he had a great talent. She was firm and demanding but fair and humble in the exercise of her office. She would be the first to take up the most menial of practical duties, and if she thought she had done something wrong in her care of her sisters, she would prostrate herself before them and ask their forgiveness. In 1574, her term of office ended. Three years later, the Discalced reform came under renewed attack, and as a result Teresa was prohibited for a time from founding new houses and was once more confined by her authorities to the Convent of the Incarnation. Those authorities wanted to make Teresa more or less disappear, but now a remarkable scene ensued. The office of prioress came open, and the same nuns who a few years previously had been so outraged at having Teresa forced upon them now wanted her back as prioress. The majority voted for her, even in the face of being excommunicated by the representative of the Carmelite order. Such was the love and admiration she had won from her sisters in the teeth of their earlier resistance.

Teresa was remarkable among mystics in her ability to live a profound contemplative life even in the midst of busy outward activity. This quality was evident throughout her life, but it was especially noteworthy in the time and circumstances of the writing of the spiritual classic, *Las Moradas,* or in English, *The Interior Castle.* Under the obedience of her superiors, Teresa wrote the work in 1577, just at the time when the Discalced reform was under grave attack and its continued existence was in peril. As the initiator of the reform, Teresa was squarely in the midst of that battle, writing letters to all parties, keeping in touch with her many foundations, and handling the awkward fallout of being elected prioress of the Incarnation against the wishes of the provincial. The actual writing of the book was accomplished in two, fourteen-day periods, during which she wrote in the early morning and late evening, taking up the business of the day during the hours in between. Yet there is no sign in her writing of those external battles and the many anxieties they brought with them. Her sisters remembered Teresa often being rapt in contemplation as she took up her pen. One of them later wrote: "Once, while she was composing the work, I entered to deliver a message, and found her so absorbed that she did not notice me; her face seemed quite illuminated and most beautiful. After having listened to me she said: 'Sit down, my child, and let me write what our Lord has told me ere I forget it,' and she went on writing with great rapidity and without stopping."[14]

The Discalced reform weathered that storm, and Teresa, now a woman of sixty-five and wracked with many illnesses, was back on the road. Despite opposition, the reform was gaining support, and there were many requests for new foundations. Teresa herself was increasingly thought of as a saint, a development that made her acutely uncomfortable. Every new foundation meant strenuous travel in all kinds of weather, a mountain of difficult administrative work, and tiresome attention to the lawsuits and false rumors inevitably initiated by the reform's opponents. The tale of that relentless reforming activity can be found in Teresa's book of *Foundations*. In the midst her many labors, Teresa's inner spirit remained in close union with God. "In some respects my soul is not really subject to the miseries of the world as it used to be," she wrote at this time. "It suffers more but it feels as if the sufferings were wounding only its garments; it does not itself lose its peace."[15] As she felt her final illness coming on in the midst of her labors, she longed once more to be at her home convent in Ávila. But death overtook her before she could return.

---

[14] Teresa of Ávila, *The Interior Castle*, The Benedictines of Stanbrook, trans.(London: Thomas Baker, 1921), 5.

[15] Shirley du Boulay, *Teresa of Ávila: An Extraordinary Life* (Katonah: Bluebridge, 1991), 245.

There might seem something incongruous in the overall shape of Teresa of Ávila's life: an eager contemplative, and yet embroiled in the affairs of the world; a person who longed for seclusion, yet who traveled constantly to all parts of Spain; an austere nun who turned her back on the things of time and sense and yet possessed to the end a spontaneous delight in friends and in the beauty of the natural world. But this combination of qualities is only incongruous if the Christian contemplative ideal is not fully understood. Teresa, like all true contemplatives, was not strictly running away from the world; rather, she was running into the arms of the world's Creator and center, God himself. In giving herself to the highest of loves, she received all things in return. She did not learn to despise loves of a lower kind; she only insisted that they be rightly ordered.

Along with her prose writings, Teresa left behind many poems. The best remembered among them was found in her breviary after she died, a testimony to her inner life of union and calm amid the distraction and trouble of a fallen but graced world.

> *Nada te turbe,*
> *Nada te espante,*
> *Todo se pasa,*
> *Dios no se muda.*
> *La paciencia*
> *Todo lo alcanza;*
> *Quien a Dios tiene*
> *Nada le falta;*
> *Solo Dios basta.*

Let nothing disturb you,
Let nothing frighten you,
All things are passing:
God never changes.
Patience gains all things.
He who has God lacks nothing;
God alone is enough.

Chapter Four

St. John of the Cross

"Where there is no love, put love and you will get back love."

> *On a night of darkness,*
> *In love's anxiety of longing kindled,*
> *O blessed chance!*
> *I left by none beheld,*
> *My house in sleep and silence stilled...*
>
> *By dark of blessed night,*
> *In secrecy, for no one saw me*
> *And I regarded nothing,*
> *My only light and guide*
> *The one that in my heart was burning...*
>
> *O night, you were the guide!*
> *O night more desirable than dawn!*
> *O dark of night you joined*
> *Beloved with belov'd one,*
> *Belov'd one in Beloved now transformed![1]*

The Renaissance of the fifteenth and sixteenth centuries was a time of a growing and increasingly exhilarating exploration of the individual human personality. Even as Europeans were

---

[1] The poetry in this chapter is translated by Lynda Nicholson in Gerald Brennan, *St. John of the Cross, His Life and Poetry* (Cambridge: Cambridge University Press, 1973), 145.

discovering new continents and setting themselves to master them, so they were discovering that darkest and most mysterious of all continents, the human soul, and with the same intrepid attitude of the conquistador, they were determined to map out and master that new terrain. This Renaissance turn to the interior, when exaggerated or uninformed by grace, could result either in abandoning the formal aspects of Christianity entirely, as happened among the more radical Protestant reformers, or in a self-absorbed introspective gaze, as with the sceptic French essayist Michel de Montaigne. For Catholic reformers who sought continuity with the great tradition, there was no interest in overthrowing the forms of Church life—the Sacraments, rites, and hierarchy—but there was a growing desire for an inner encounter with Christ that would correspond to those forms and deepen the life of faith. Much of the zeal of the Catholic Reformation was rooted in a renewed cultivation of the interior life. The Spiritual Exercises of Ignatius were a noteworthy expression of this development. In Teresa of Ávila and John of the Cross, the inner ascent to God reached extraordinary heights.

The stanzas at the head of the chapter are from John of the Cross's poem "The Dark Night." Despite the slim number of his poems, John of the Cross has been granted a place in the first rank of Spanish poets, both for the quality and the variety of his work. Yet what is most remarkable about this poem is not the skill of its writer, but the circumstances under which it was written. John penned this lyrical love song to God just after escaping from a kind of living hell—imprisoned, betrayed, tortured, ignorant of the future, seemingly forgotten and abandoned. What emerges from John's life and teaching is a truth worth pondering: that it was not in spite of, but rather because of, his horrific circumstances that John was so taken by the love of God. In his poetry, in his prose writings, and preeminently in the shape of his life, John points to the mystery of the redemptive nature of the Crucifixion. He was intensely a man of the Cross; and because of that he was an ardent lover and an effective reformer.

The theme of suffering with Christ for the sake of humanity runs like a silken thread through the lives and teaching of all the saints of the Catholic Reformation. From her first conversion to the end of her life, Catherine of Genoa's consuming desire was to unite herself to Christ's sufferings in order to bring goodness to the world. Thomas More was brought to prison and death for his adherence to the Faith, a development that was of a piece with the rest of his life. He once said to his children: "We may not look at our pleasure to go to Heaven in featherbeds; it is not the way, for our Lord Himself went thither with great pain, and by many tribulations, which was the path wherein He walked thither, and the servant may not look to be in better case than his Master."[2] Ignatius Loyola embraced the same attitude: "If God causes you to suffer much, it is a sign that He has great designs for you, and that He certainly intends to make you a saint. And if you wish to become a great saint, entreat Him yourself to give you much opportunity for suffering; for there is no wood better to kindle the fire of holy love than the cross, which Christ used for His own great sacrifice of boundless charity." Ignatius's great disciple Francis Xavier was constantly on the lookout for ways to suffer for Christ. Once on a sea voyage from Malacca to India, his ship was caught in a terrific monsoon, the worst he had ever seen, and all aboard

[2] Roper, *Life of Sir Thomas More*, Pt. 1.

thought the ship was going down. Amid the fear and fury of the storm, Xavier's eyes were on the way his suffering might be a gain for the Kingdom. He later wrote, "I begged our Lord during the storm that, if I came out of it alive, it might only be to endure others as bad or worse for His greater service."[3] The joyful Philip Neri was of the same school: "The greatness of our love for God must be tested by the desire we have of suffering for his love....Nothing more glorious can happen to a Christian, than to suffer for Christ. There is no surer or clearer proof of the love of God than adversity."[4] St. Anthony Mary Claret never complained about the numerous trials he endured, including fourteen attempts on his life; he thought it a necessary part of God's saving action. He once wrote: "Christian perfection consists in three things: praying heroically, working heroically, and suffering heroically." Teresa of Ávila, full of interest in all aspects of life as she was, once wrote to her sisters: "I want to make clear to you in what God's will consists. Think not that it is to give you pleasures, riches....He loves you too well to give you these things. Consider what the Father gave Him whom He loved above all—suffering, the Cross— and you will understand what His will is. So long as we are in this world, these are His gifts. He gives them to us according to the love he bears us."[5] As with these other saints, so with John of the Cross. One of his "Maxims of Love" goes, "Love consists not in feeling great things but in having great detachment and in suffering for the Beloved."[6]

---

[3] Brodrick, *St. Francis Xavier*, 302.

[4] Pietro Bacci, *The Life of St. Philip Neri*, F.W. Faber, trans. (London: Richardson, 1847), 308.

[5] Teresa of Avila, *The Way of Perfection*, Ch. 32.

[6] *The Collected Works of John of the Cross*, Kieran Kavanaugh and Otilio Rodriguez, trans. (Washington: ICS Publications, 1979), 676.

John's Early Life

John de Yepes y Álvarez (to give him his original name) seemed marked out for suffering from his childhood. John was born in a town near Ávila in 1542. His father, Gonzalo, was from a wealthy merchant family (like Teresa of Ávila's father, probably of Jewish origin), who married a poor orphan girl named Catalina Álvarez. Gonzalo's family was appalled by the match and they disowned Gonzalo, who was forced to take up the economically unstable trade of his wife and become a weaver. Three sons came of the marriage, John being the youngest. Shortly after John was born, his father Gonzalo died, leaving Catalina to patch a life together as best she could for herself and her three young children. She moved from place to place plying her trade, eventually settling in the city of Medina del Campo. From his childhood on, John knew well what it meant to be poor, to go hungry and be poorly clothed, and to face the future without financial security. The experience did not make him bitter, but it gave him a deep compassion for the poor and suffering. It also toughened him; his later endurance of bodily austerities was learned in a hard school from a young age.

Catalina found that she could not support all her children; at the age of ten, John was boarded out at an orphanage, the Colegio de la Doctrina. John was an intelligent youth, deeply reserved, ardent but silent. During his teens he supported himself by working as a nurse in a large hospital, where he developed another quality that lasted to the end of his life: a ready sympathy for the sick. At the age of seventeen he attended the newly founded Jesuit College in Medina, where he remained for four years. At twenty-one he took the Carmelite habit under the name John of St. Matthew. He then spent three years at the University of Salamanca; at age twenty-five he was ordained a priest. It can be seen that John benefited from the new reforms that were making their way in the Church. He was given an excellent education by the Jesuits in the Christian humanist tradition, augmented at Salamanca under the influence of the humanist scholar Francisco de Vitoria, an education that emphasized firm knowledge of the Scriptures and the study of the Church Fathers. Salamanca was also home to a revival of the theology of Thomas Aquinas. These various influences—familiarity with the Scriptures, knowledge of the Fathers, appreciation of Thomas's theology, all brought into harmony in an atmosphere of prayer and sacrament—were evident in John's later work, along with a more humble delight in vernacular love songs learned among the weavers of his youth.

Unlike Teresa of Ávila, John was almost never autobiographical in his writings, so we have little detail concerning his early life. But it seems that he had settled on a vocation to the priesthood and to the contemplative life very early. He had always been a devout youth, and already during his university days at Salamanca, when not attending lectures he would study for long hours at his desk in his bare cell, refusing to join his companions in recreation or light conversation. He spent a large part of every night in prayer and was beginning to practice a severe ascetic regimen: he fasted rigorously and would whip himself to the point of drawing blood.

In 1567, the year he was ordained a priest, John met Teresa. Five years previously, Teresa had founded the Discalced Convent of St. Joseph, and she was now looking for likely priests of the order who could effect the same kind of reform among the friars. John was feeling drawn to a life of contemplation and austerity deeper than the Carmelites then offered and was thinking of joining the Carthusians. Teresa convinced him to stay with the Carmelites and to help her initiate a reform among the male branch. Teresa wrote to her sisters, "Thanks be to God, daughters, I have found a friar and a half to start the Reform with."[7] It was a remark with a vein of humor in it, because John might have seemed only half a friar. He was under five feet tall and slight in build. But he had the vivid intensity of a laser beam. "Though he is small of stature," Teresa wrote, "I believe he is great in the eyes of God. ... There is not a friar but speaks well of him for he leads a life of great penitence, though he entered upon it so recently. But the Lord seems to be leading him by the hand."[8] John's readiness to join the Discalced reform came with a characteristic condition: that he would not have to wait too long. As it happened, he did not have to wait long. He returned to Salamanca for one last year of study, and then in the fall of 1568 he went to Duruelo, where Teresa had secured a small dwelling. There he and one other friar began the first priory of the Discalced reform. He took the name John of the Cross.

During the next eight years, John was busy furthering the reform. Five of those years he spent as chaplain at the Convent of the Incarnation, where he was confessor to Teresa. This was the period of their closest collaboration. Teresa and John were not naturally sympathetic personalities. In addition to being twice his age, Teresa—that most human of saints—preferred a dash of charm and playful wit in those close to her, and John was quiet and very serious. But Teresa understood John's worth, and later insisted that she never

[7] Brenan, *St. John of the Cross*, 22.
[8] *Ibid*, 13, 23.

had so good a spiritual director. "I have sometimes been vexed with him," she wrote, "but we have never seen the least imperfection in him."[9] For John, the time with Teresa was one of gaining experience in pastoring souls and of a deepening life of prayer. While he could not have been called Teresa's student, he gained much from her example and from her experience of mystical contemplation.

Persecution

The story of the Carmelite reform is a tangled one, fraught with the confusion of overlapping jurisdictions and bedeviled by human weakness and imprudence. But it follows a pattern important to understand for the reform of the Church. It seems a rule that the stiffest opposition to the work of God comes, not from the unbelieving world, but from elements within the Church. At first sight this can seem anomalous; but in the light of God's preferred manner of saving the world it makes more sense. "The Lord has chosen Zion," sings the psalmist, "he has desired it for his habitation: 'This is my resting place for ever'" (Ps 132:13–14). Once God had initiated salvation history by gathering a people to himself who were to be salt and light to the world, that people and their history emerged as the center of the world's narrative, the unique stage upon which the human drama would be enacted. First the Chosen People of Israel and then the Christian Church became by necessity the main theater of spiritual warfare. Jesus's most difficult opponents were not the general populace, but the Pharisees and the chief priests; Paul was far more concerned about false teachers than about pagan unbelievers; and down the centuries the fiercest

---

[9] *Ibid*, 13.

battles that Christians have waged have been with other Church members, often involving bishops and members of religious orders. Efforts to renew the Church have been most strenuously opposed by factions within the Church itself. Teresa of Ávila once alluded to this reality: "The way of true religion is so little used that friars or nuns who begin truly to follow their calling have more to fear from members of their own communities than from all the devils."[10] For reform to take root there is always a need for the endurance of Christlike suffering by some of the Church's members at the hands of others within the Christian community. John of the Cross seemed set apart for just this purpose; he exemplifies what it means to be offered with Christ as a sacrificial victim for the renewal of the Church.

The storm that was gathering against the Discalced reform intensified in 1576 when Juan Bautista Rubeo, the same Carmelite general who had so warmly encouraged Teresa to make new foundations, suddenly turned against the reform and sought to end the growth and even the existence of Discalced friaries and convents, fearing that the reform was introducing deep divisions into the Carmelite order. This began a serious conflict, as the Carmelite general and his representatives took measures to curtail or to end the Discalced reform, while the papal nuncio, backed by the King of Spain, continued to support it. The struggle led to Teresa's "house arrest" at the Convent of the Incarnation. A decisive moment in the conflict came when the papal nuncio, a certain Nicolo Ormaneto who had been Charles Borromeo's vicar-general in Milan and an unfailing friend to the reform, died, and a new nuncio, Filippo Sega, who was dead set against reform,

---

[10] Teresa of Avila, *Autobiography*, 52.

was appointed. Sega had once referred to Teresa as "a restless gad-about, a disobedient and contumacious woman."[11] With Ormaneto's protection removed, the opponents of the Discalced reform grew bolder. Among various measures taken, they determined to act against John of the Cross, one of the first of the Discalced friars.

John had been living in a hermitage in Ávila with another Discalced friar in his capacity as confessor at the Convent of the Incarnation. He was now commanded by Carmelite authorities to return to his original monastery and to stop following the Discalced constitutions. Upon resisting this move, John and his friar companion were apprehended by a posse of Carmelite monks and armed men and were spirited away—where, no one knew. John was taken first to the priory in Ávila, where he was flogged. He was then taken by unfrequented roads in the middle of the night, blindfolded so he would not know where he was going, to the priory at Toledo. There he was brought before a tribunal and accused of insubordination for not obeying the order to leave his post as confessor at Ávila and for insisting on living according to the Discalced reform. He was told that if he submitted to the ruling of the tribunal, his offense would be overlooked, and he would be given a high office in the Carmelite order. Nonetheless, John remained firm, saying that he had no authority to leave his post since it had been assigned to him by the papal representative, and he had taken a vow to follow the Discalced constitutions—a vow that he was not free to break. The tribunal found him guilty of rebellion and contumacy, and he was condemned to imprisonment for as long as the general of the order might determine. As soon

[11] du Boulay, *Teresa of Avila,* 216.

as John had disappeared, Teresa had written to King Philip and to whatever influential bishops she knew, registering her anxiety about his situation. "I don't know how it is," she wrote, "that that saint is so unfortunate that no one remembers him."[12] But no one knew where John was, and nothing could be done.

For two months John was held in the prison cell of the priory. But for fear that he might escape the cell, the friars found a more secure spot. They imprisoned John in a small room, six by ten feet, that had previously been used as a closet. The room had a small slit high in the wall by which a little light could enter the cell. John could read his Office only by standing on a stool and holding his breviary above his head, and then only at the middle of the day. His bed was a board on the floor, covered by two old rugs. The room was freezing cold during the winter months when John was first captured. It then became swelteringly hot and stuffy as the summer months drew on. He was given no opportunity to wash and was allowed no change of clothing, and so was devoured by lice. His food consisted of a few scraps of bread and an occasional sardine, tossed on the floor of his cell. He soon contracted dysentery and grew afraid that the friars were attempting to poison him. John's bucket would purposely be left in his cell for days, creating such a stench that it made him vomit. His tunic, clotted with blood from beatings, began to putrefy, and worms bred in it. Never a person of vigorous health, this treatment over a period of many months made John weak and emaciated and brought him close to death.

On fast days John was brought to the refectory and made to kneel while the friars took their meal. An early biography

[12] Brenan, *St. John of the Cross*, 29.

based on firsthand accounts related the kind of admonish-
ment given him by the prior of the house on these occasions:

> If you wished to be good, what hindered you from remaining in
> an order that has produced so many friars who have been good
> and holy? But you, hypocrite, were not aiming at being a saint, but
> only at being thought one: not at the edification of the people but
> at the satisfaction of your own self-esteem. Look at him, brothers,
> this miserable, wretched little friar, scarcely good enough to be a
> convent porter! He seeks to reform others when what he needs is to
> reform himself. Now bare your shoulders: it is on them that we will
> write the rules of the new reform.[13]

Then each of the friars would strike him in turn with a cane.
John bore the punishment in silence, which seemed only to
aggravate his persecutors the more.

During this time of imprisonment John was held in
solitary confinement. He was allowed to speak to no one; the
one person he regularly saw, the friar who served as his jailor,
treated him with contempt. The friars would sometimes
converse outside his room with the purpose of allowing him
to overhear their talk. They would say to one another that the
prisoner would never be let out, and that all the Discalced
monks and nuns had abandoned both him and the reform.
All of this caused John great distress of mind.

After six months of this treatment, John experienced a
slight relief. A younger friar from a different priory became
his jailor, and he treated his prisoner with more compassion.
The new jailor found John a clean tunic and gave him a needle
and thread with which to mend his habit. He provided him
with pen and ink for writing, and an oil lamp by which he
could read his Office. He would sometimes leave the door of

---

[13] *Ibid*, 30–1.

the cell open to let in a bit of light and air. During these times John was able to get out of his cell and to better ascertain his whereabouts in the monastery.

For nine months John was made to endure this crucifixion of suffering and isolation. He came to think that he would never get out of his cell alive. Then, according to one account, he received a vision from the Virgin Mary telling him that he was soon to escape his time of imprisonment. Emboldened by the vision, he decided to make the attempt. The Carmelite priory was built against the city wall. He calculated that there was a place from which he could escape over the wall if he cut up the rugs in his cell and tied the strands together to make a long rope. On the night of August 14, the eve of the Feast of the Assumption, John made his rope and, having earlier loosened the screws of the prison door, opened his cell and slipped out past two sleeping friars. By the light of a full moon he tied his rope to a railing and slid down, jumping the remaining ten feet. He then found himself trapped in the enclosure of a Franciscan convent; but he found a place where the plaster had broken loose and so was able to climb the wall and get into the street. He was now lost in a city he did not know in the middle of the night. He took shelter in a house until morning, and then asked the way to the Discalced convent. He found it, rang the bell, and spoke to the extern sister. It was the first anyone had heard of him for almost a year.

Upon his arrival at the convent, John was so thin and sickly that he seemed an image of death. He could speak only in a whisper and could hardly stand. The nuns, knowing the danger he was in, took him inside their enclosure. When the friars at the Carmelite priory discovered his escape, as they soon did, they went ranging through the city looking for him. They came to the Discalced convent and searched the grounds, but they did not dare to enter the enclosure. The nuns were soon able to get John into the hands of a wealthy nobleman, a friend to the reform, who gave him protection and a place to recuperate.

John's indomitable spirit can be seen in his response to his new freedom. Among the first things he did upon entering the Discalced convent was to read to the sisters the poems he had written during his imprisonment. It is an astonishing scene: a scarecrow of a man, at death's door, famished, filthy, beaten to a pulp, and starved of human companionship, does not ask for food or drink or a safe haven. Instead he only wants to speak of the goodness and beauty of God; his keenest desire is to share his love for the One who came to him in the darkness, who revealed himself most clearly and alluringly in the midst of crucifixion.

John's Mystical Writings

After his escape from prison, John made his way to the south of Spain, to the friary of El Calvario. A short time later, once his health had been more or less restored, he was elected prior of the house. Nearby was a convent of Discalced nuns under the direction of one of the strongest personalities among Teresa's spiritual daughters, Ana de Jesús. Ana was on the lookout for a confessor for her sisters, and like many who encountered John, she was not at first impressed. She wrote to Teresa for advice on how to find a suitable priest for the position. Teresa wrote back: "It has really amused me, daughter, to see you complaining with so little reason when you have with you my Father Fray Juan de la Cruz, that divine and heavenly man. I assure you, my daughter, that since he left these parts

I have not found another like him in the whole of Castile, nor one who inspires souls with such fervor on their journey to heaven."[14] Ana took Teresa's advice and enlisted John as confessor. It was a happy decision, since it was in caring for the nuns at this convent of Beas and explaining to them the principles of contemplative prayer that John wrote the best known of his prose works, *The Ascent of Mount Carmel* and *The Dark Night of the Soul*.

John's teaching on the mystical life can be best understood as the outworking of a passionate relationship of love. When he tried to communicate the sources of his spiritual vision, he could only express his ideas fully in love poetry modeled on the biblical Song of Songs. Even in his prose works he began with poetry; the whole of his lengthy volumes are extensive explanations of what the poetry means. Yet there is nothing sappy or sentimental in John's way of love. The road he mapped out could be intimidating in its relentless determination to allow nothing to get in the way of that highest of loves. "Set me as a seal upon your heart, as a seal upon your arm; for love is strong as death, jealousy is cruel as the grave. Its flashes are flashes of fire, a most vehement flame" (Sg 8:6). These verses point to the kind of love one meets in the writings of John: a love as strong as death, a flame of consuming fire, a jealousy that will brook no rival. Yet John himself was a very gentle soul, and he handled his spiritual charges with great sensitivity. "The holier a man is," he once wrote, "the gentler he is and the less scandalized by the faults of others, because he knows the weak condition of man."[15]

---

[14] *Ibid*, 44.
[15] *Ibid*, 24.

One of John's most potent images for describing the purifying effects of God's love was his extended comparison of the soul with a log of wood in a hot fire.

> Fire, when applied to wood, first dehumidifies it, dispelling all moisture and making it give off any water it contains. Then it gradually turns the wood black, makes it dark and ugly, and even causes it to emit a bad odor. By drying out the wood, the fire brings to light and expels all those ugly and dark accidents which are contrary to fire. Finally, by heating and enkindling it from without, the fire transforms the wood into itself and makes it as beautiful as it is itself.[16]

According to John, a similar process occurred when the fire of divine love began to enkindle the soul.

> Before transforming the soul, [divine love] purges it of all contrary qualities. It produces blackness and darkness and brings to the fore the soul's ugliness; thus the soul seems worse than before and unsightly and abominable. This divine purge stirs up all the foul and vicious humors of which the soul was never before aware; never did it realize there was so much evil in itself, since these humors were so deeply rooted.[17]

This experience of purification could be very painful; it was an aspect of what John called the "dark night." But the point of the purgation was to allow the fullness of divine love to take full possession of the soul. This was why John called this night not only dark, but also "more desirable than the dawn." John then went on to describe the effects of the dark night:

> God makes the soul die to all that He is not, so that when it is stripped and flayed of its old skin, He may clothe it anew. Its youth

---

[16] John of the Cross, *The Dark Night of the Soul*, in *The Collected Works*, 350.
[17] *Ibid.*

is renewed like the eagle's, clothed in the new man. This renovation is an illumination of the human intellect with supernatural light so that it becomes divine, united with the divine; an informing of the will with love of God so that it is no longer less than divine and loves in no other way than divinely, united and made one with the divine will and love. And thus this soul will be a soul of heaven, more divine than human.[18]

This possibility of becoming a "partaker of the divine nature" (2 Pt 1:4) was the dizzyingly high vision that had captured John of the Cross, and upon which he focused the whole of his formidable energy of mind and soul. Something of that vision is caught in John's poem, "A Quarry of Love":

> *Bent on an enterprise of love,*
> *And not in lack of hope,*
> *I flew so high, so high above*
> *I caught my quarry on the wing.*
> *As I rose to the higher reaches,*
> *Dazzled, blinded was my vision,*
> *And in an utter darkness won*
> *The hardest of my victories;*
> *I took a blind, unknowing plunge*
> *Because the venture was for love,*
> *And went so high, so high above*
> *I caught my quarry on the wing.*[19]

John's Last Days

The last days of John of the Cross were in keeping with the cruciform shape of his life. John seldom reported anything of his own mystical experiences; but once he related to his

---

[18] *Ibid*, 361.
[19] Brenan, 175.

brother an encounter with Christ. One evening as he was praying before the cross, Christ had spoken to him, saying: "Fray Juan, ask what favor you will of me and I will grant it in return for the services you have done me." To this John replied: "Lord make me to suffer and be despised for your sake."[20] John's prayer of love for his crucified Lord was heard and answered.

By 1588 the Discalced reform had gained a measure of independence, and its existence and growth were now secured. Teresa had gone to her reward, and John had continued the work of founding new houses and of acting as a beloved prior and spiritual director to many in the reform. The new Discalced congregation now elected Nicolas Doria, of the powerful Genoese family, as its first vicar-general. Doria was a strong personality who came to his post with many innovations in mind, including a desire to centralize the government of the Discalced congregations. When John spoke up for what many considered the essence of the Discalced reform as it had been pioneered by Teresa, he ran afoul of the new vicar-general, who determined to marginalize him and if possible to disgrace him. In 1591 John was stripped of whatever responsibilities he had held and was sent to an isolated and distant friary at a place called La Peñuela. When some among his brothers urged him to lodge protests against this unfair treatment, he refused to defend himself. While at La Peñuela he soon caught a fever, and he died even as his enemies were gathering libelous testimonies against him, hoping to report him to the Inquisition. He was not yet fifty years old. Moved by love to the last, on his deathbed John asked one of his Carmelite brothers to read him verses out

[20] *Ibid*, 66.

of the Song of Songs. The time had come for the exile to go home; the day had arrived for the eager lover to embrace in its fullness what he had so ardently desired and so zealously pursued through the course of his life.

> *Entrádose ha la Esposa*
> *En el ameno huerto deseado,*
> *Y a su sabor reposa*
> *El cuello reclinado*
> *sobre los dulces brazos del Amado.*

> *She has entered in, the Bride,*
> *To the long desired and pleasant garden,*
> *And at her ease she lies,*
> *Her neck reclined*
> *To rest upon the Loved One's gentle arms.*

(from "Spiritual Canticle")[21]

---

[21] *Ibid*, 214.

Afterword

It was December of the year 1531. The previous fifteen years had sent seismic shocks through the Church and European society. Under Luther in Germany and Zwingli in Switzerland, the Protestant Reformation was unsettling long-standing ideas and putting the unity of the Church at risk. Thomas More was about to resign his chancellorship in England under the pressure of Henry's Act of Succession. Rome had been devastated a few years earlier by imperial armies, and Vienna was about to endure its second siege by the armies of Suleiman, the invading Turkish sultan. Ignatius Loyola and John Calvin were at the University of Paris, unknown to each other, their plans still germinating. Spain had conquered the Aztec Empire ten years earlier and was securing its new American possessions.

In the midst of these powerful personalities and earth-shaking events, a native of Mexico, a simple man who had been baptized seven years earlier and received the name Juan Diego, experienced something strange and wonderful as he was walking in an out-of-the-way place by the hill of Tepeyac. He heard music and singing coming from the top of the hill, and then heard his name called. He ascended the hill, and there was greeted by the vision of a beautiful woman who identified herself as Mary, the Mother of God. This was the beginning of the famous story of the Virgin of Guadalupe—the Blessed Mother who came as a mestiza princess, who spoke both Nahuatl and Spanish, and who imprinted her image on the *tilma* of Juan Diego. The apparition, and Juan Diego's faithfulness to the Virgin's message, opened the floodgates of conversion and laid the foundation of the Mexican church. Within fifteen years, some nine million native Mexicans had been baptized. It was a monumental step in the renewal and growth of the Church and caught the imagination, not only of Mexico but also of Europe; the image of Guadalupe was flying from the masthead of the Genoese captain Andrea Doria's flagship at the battle of Lepanto.

A great deal might be said about the significance of Our Lady of Guadalupe in the history of the Church and the world. For this discussion, it is important to note that the one who was evangelizing and renewing the Church's life was the Blessed Virgin herself. It is a reminder about where the initiative lies in all matters of Church governance and growth. The Church belongs to Christ; it is his Body, and he rules it according to his wisdom and his plans. God has dignified humanity by allowing us to participate in his life and mission. But our part is always subordinate to his and is effective only when it is ruled by his initiative. All the energy of the greatest saints would count for nothing if it were not expended in cooperation with the action of Christ.

G.K. Chesterton once wrote:

> The faith has not only often died but it has often died of old age. It has not only been often killed but it has often died a natural death; in the sense of coming to a natural and necessary end. It is obvious that it has survived the most savage and the most universal persecutions from the shock of the Diocletian fury to the shock of the French Revolution. But it has a more strange and even a more weird tenacity; it has survived not only war but peace. It has not only died often but degenerated often and decayed often; it has

survived its own weakness and even its own surrender.... It was supposed to have been withered up at last in the dry light of the Age of Reason; it was supposed to have disappeared ultimately in the earthquake of the Age of Revolution. Science explained it away; and it was still there. History disinterred it in the past; and it appeared suddenly in the future. Today it stands once more in our path; and even as we watch it, it grows.[1]

The "weird tenacity" that Chesterton writes of touches on the Church's dual nature. The human aspect of the Church is subject to all the failings and weaknesses of a fallen humanity. If we look only at that human side of things we can be fooled into thinking that they exhaust the Church's hopes and resources. But because the heart of the Church is in Heaven, because the Church's most potent membership is already perfected in the presence of God, because though she is an ancient society the Church is also the newest thing on the face of the earth by the presence of the Holy Spirit within her, it becomes clear that supernatural reform and revival are natural to her life. The reform of the sixteenth century, spurred by an array of exceptional personalities, was an impressive example of this process, of divine initiative enlisting the cooperation of willing men and women—saints— for the regeneration of the Church's life. So it was then; so it is now. The last hundred years or so have seen yet another array of remarkable saints: Padre Pio and Mother Teresa; Maximilian Kolbe and Teresa Benedicta of the Cross; Pius X, John XXIII, and John Paul II; Faustina Kowalska and Thérèse of Lisieux.

---

[1] G.K. Chesterton, *The Everlasting Man*, Part 2, Ch. 6.

Their lives and example, along with many others, are indicators of the continuing heavenly initiative taken by Christ as he cares for his Body. They also make clear the lines along which the reform and renewal of the Church in our day will proceed. It is once again the saints who provide the key to understanding the work of God in our time. As we imitate the saints in their imitation of Christ, we can once again expect the regenerating life of the Holy Spirit to renew and reform the Church.

TAKE A PILGRIMAGE
WITH SIX HEROES OF THE CATHOLIC REFORMATION

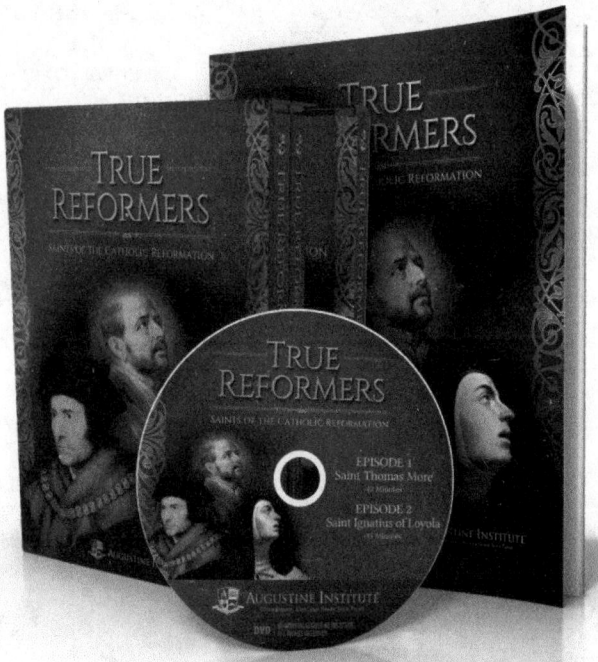

In this 6-part video series, learn about the leaders who led the Church's rebirth from the ashes of confusion caused by the Protestant Reformation.

The saints of the Catholic Reformation show us just how powerful—and beautiful—is the human heart's free response to God's generous grace.

FORMED®

THE CATHOLIC FAITH. ON DEMAND.

Discover the site that gathers more Catholic content in one place.

One convenient website

Save the time you used to spend searching and find the Catholic content you want. On demand and available when you are.

High quality

You'll always find beautiful, trustworthy, Catholic content.

New and updated regularly

Discover new and fresh materials every week.

More choices

Easily choose from a wide range of content options: movies, ebooks, audio talks, and video studies.

Go to formed.org for a free trial!